T0372221

PALETTE
mini

MONOTONE

Published and distributed by
viction:workshop ltd.

viction:ary™

viction:workshop ltd.
Unit C, 7/F, Seabright Plaza, 9-23 Shell Street,
North Point, Hong Kong
Url: victionary.com
Email: we@victionary.com
🅕 @victionworkshop
🅞 @victionworkshop
Bē @victionary
🅟 @victionary

Edited and produced by viction:ary

Creative direction by Victor Cheung
Book design by viction:workshop ltd.
Typeset in NB International Pro from Neubau

Third Edition

ISBN 978-988-74628-6-6
Printed and bound in China

PREFACE

Although monotones may sound monotonous or one-dimensional, they can actually be used to add depth and dimension to design work when wielded by the right pair of hands. Also known as a monochromatic colour, a monotone typically refers to a single base hue but includes the shades, tints and tones derived from that hue to form an elegant palette that is easy to the eye. The trick lies in picking the foundation wisely, depending on the type of project it is going to be applied onto, and then finding a contrasting colour to prevent the final visual from sinking into the background. For example, promotional materials that need to draw attention from viewers could do with more vibrant hues versus packaging, which could play with more subtle pigments.

The variety of projects in this book showcase the compelling array of ways with which monotones can be utilised for different purposes to create a lasting impression. For Ken Lo's 'Walking in the Dream' exhibition (PP. 096-101), a beautiful blush of pink anchors the key visual of a fluffy pillow, which is emblematic of the exhibition theme. The same pink shade is applied across all the communication materials for the show, which features a mix of illustrations and photography to convey a sense of dreamy whimsicality. In Futura's branding work for SOY, a high-end

Asian restaurant in Doha (PP. 128-135), the studio was inspired by the name itself to represent it as more than just an ingredient, which is one of the most ancient and traditional staples found in Asian cuisine. Instead, based on the idea of primitivism, the team created a graphic system around copper and rose gold to narrate the beginnings of Asian culture. The refined end-result balances the raw and the sophisticated. TUKATA, a lifestyle brand that sets out to present new takes on ordinary objects, was driven to change the way people perceive the shade of blue that was being used to 'represent' the COVID-19 pandemic in 2020 (PP. 490-497). To disassociate it from the negative connotations of disease and depression, the team launched a series of products to encourage people to remember its pre-COVID-19 perceptions, like the colour of the ocean or freshness, and find new joy.

Beyond branding, monotones in interior design may not be easy to apply, but they can be used to create striking spaces that are also calming. To prevent them from looking sterile, the designer can use textures, patterns and elements to add warmth and a sense of welcome. In 2014, Japanese design office id's work on SUMIYOSHIDO Kampo Lounge, an acupuncture clinic where oriental treatments are administered, featured a fresh mint green shade to express the plant-based world of herbal medicine (PP. 342-351). By painting the waiting/seating area in a single hue, the team managed to soften the angles of the furniture and fittings – a soothing ambience that was further enhanced by the uniform white of the treatment area. The same colours were extended to the clinic's branding on print for cohesion. For MOSS, a boutique hotel in Hobart (PP. 324-329), Studio Ongarato considered every design touchpoint to merge nature into the brand experience to create a rich cultural retreat that visitors can immerse themselves in. Embodying travellers' existing perceptions of Tasmania as a refuge of the wilderness, the green artefacts that were curated for its visual identity reflect the shade as the colour of life, renewal and the environment.

By keeping a palette to a minimum, there is still potential to create variety out of singularity and out of ordinary outcomes with maximum impact. All it goes to show is that there is no limit as to how creative one can be – if only one dares to try.

info@helvetiatrust.com

dufourstrasse 40
st. gallen, switzerland

tel +41 55.280.50.00
fax +41 55.280.60.66

w   helvetiatrust.com

grand opening
groß premiere

zürich
switzerland

HelvetiaTrus

holding & fina

zürich	st. gallen	mexico city
dufourstrasse 30	dufourstrasse 40	puebla 114
zürich, switzerland	st. gallen, switzerland	col. roma norte, méxico

grand opening
groß premiere

zürich
switzerland

info@helvetiatrust.com

dufourptrasse 40
st. gallen, switzerland

tel   +41 58.280.50.00
fax +41 58.280.60.66

w   helvetiatrust.com

HelvetiaTrust
holding & financial

zürich
dufourptrasse 30
zürich, switzerland

st. gallen
dufourptrasse 40
st. gallen, switzerland

mexico city
puebla 114
col. roma norte, méxico

013

"I only use red, which is the colour of blood and matches the posters' theme. It's also easier to catch people's eyes this way."

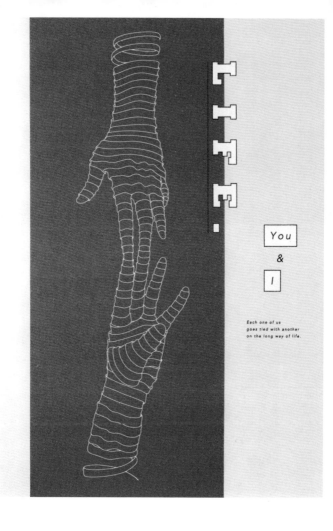

LIFE.

You
&
I

Each one of us
goes tied with another
on the long way of life.

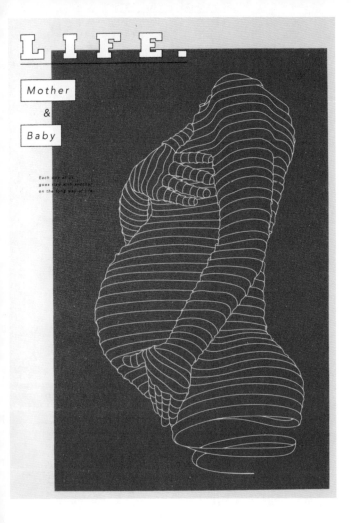

L I F E.

Mother
&
Baby

Each day of us
goes tied with another
on the long way of life

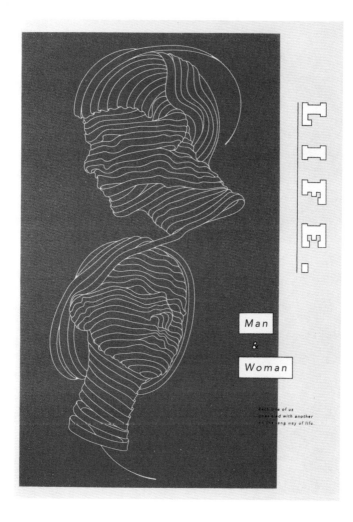

L.I.F.E.

Man

&

Woman

Each one of us
goes clad with another
as the lifelong way of life.

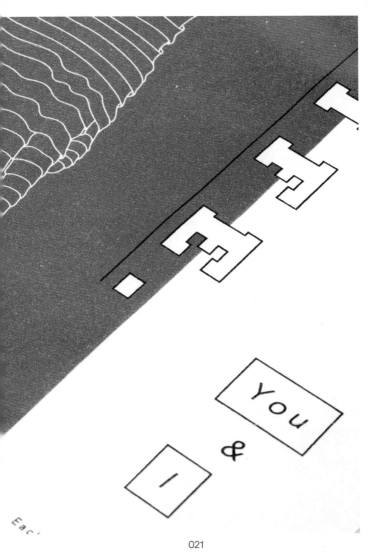

You

&

I

Good people will bring The Canteen to life each day. We want our ten retail partners to represent the pick of Sydney's colourful, high calibre food scene and to transform The Canteen into the city's most outstanding collection of casual eateries.

Our signage and printed collateral is designed to reflect the strong collaboration between The Canteen and its retail partners. Using a refined yet flexible design system, we will showcase your brand in a clear and positive way that together shows us in our best light.

"Ask not what you can do for your country. Ask what's for lunch."

— Orson Welles.

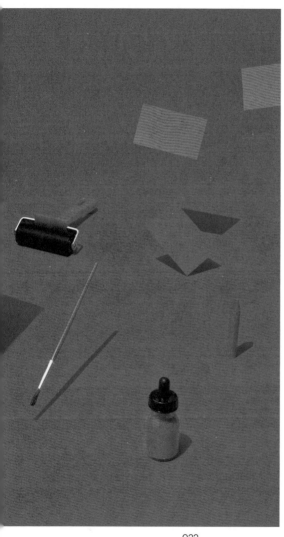

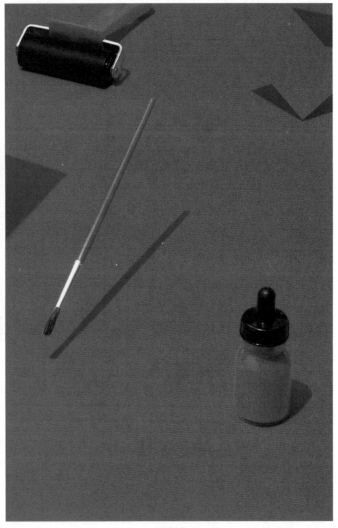

lean app...
...at equals fir...
...ting without the b...
...r cutting edge techolog...
...modern roster of talent...
...cated production team is here...
...support you in winning / creative...
video marketing that impact with
multiplied value over dollars spent.

Tim Nagle

Executive Producer / Founder

100 W...
North S...

APOSTLE

DIGITAL

APOSTLE

DIGITAL

APOSTLE

DIGITAL

Tim Nagle

Ex

M +61 423 720 100
E   tim@apostledigital.com
W apsti.co

Executive Producer Founder

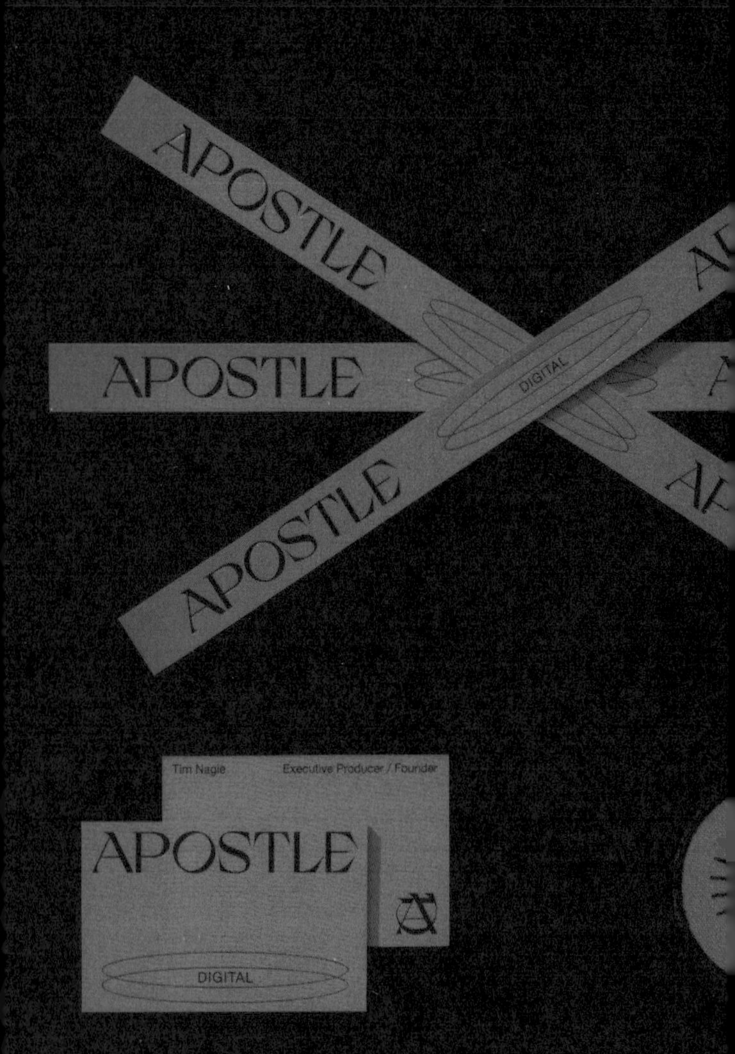
APOSTLE
APOSTLE
APOSTLE
DIGITAL
Tim Nagle
Executive Producer / Founder
APOSTLE
DIGITAL

APOSTLE

We specialise in high quality video production with kick-ass content strategy to attract new customers. We offer the highest quality video production that places heart into the creative & intelligence into the targeted strategy resulting in super star ROI for the brands we partner with. Based out of Sydney we offer a nimble, fast & lean approach for our clients that equals first class video marketing without the bloat. We sport cutting edge techology and our modern roster of talent dedicated production team is here to support you in winning / creative video marketing that impact with multiplied value over dollars spent.

Tim Nagle   Executive Producer / Founder

We specialise in high quality video production with kick-ass content strategy to attract new customers. We offer the highest quality video production that places heart into the creative & intelligence into the targeted strategy, resulting in super star ROI for the brands we partner with. Based out of Sydney we offer our clients that equals first class a nimble, fast & lean approach for video marketing without the bloat. We sport cutting edge technology and our modern roster of talent dedicated production team is here to support you in winning / creative video marketing that impact with multiplied value over dollars spent

We specialise in high quality video production with kick-ass content strategy to attract new customers. We offer the highest quality video production that places heart into the creative & intelligence into the targeted strategy, resulting in super star ROI for the brands we partner with. Based out of Sydney we offer our clients that equals first class a nimble, fast & lean approach for video marketing without the bloat. We sport cutting edge technology and our modern roster of talent dedicated production team is here to support you in winning / creative video marketing that impact with multiplied value over dollars spent

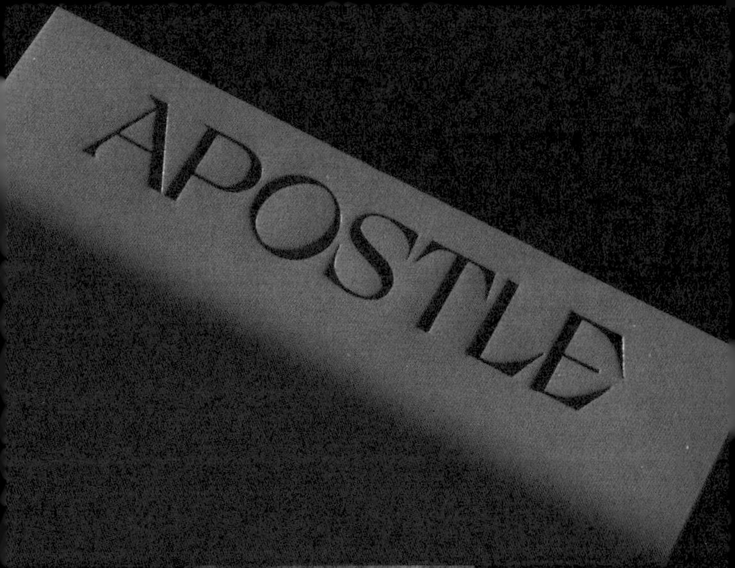
APOSTLE
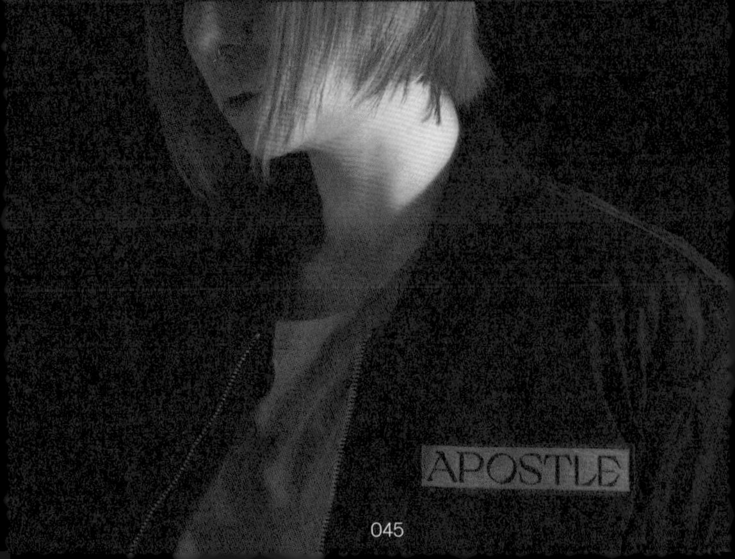
APOSTLE

ITS
THE
THOUGHT
THAT
YOU'LL
COUNT

IT'S
THE
THOUGHT
THAT
YOU'LL
COUNT

Department of Fine and Applied Arts, Kyoto University of Art and Design
Graduation Exhibition Catalogue　2012

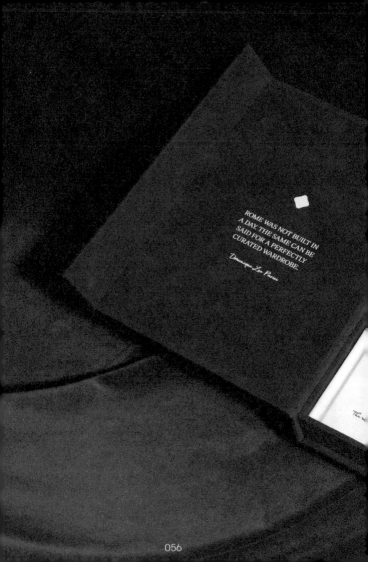

ROME WAS NOT BUILT IN
A DAY. THE SAME CAN BE
SAID FOR A PERFECTLY
CURATED WARDROBE.

Dominique Lee Paris

THE WARDROBE

MAKEOVER

CHALLENGE

personal style and wardrobe organisation.

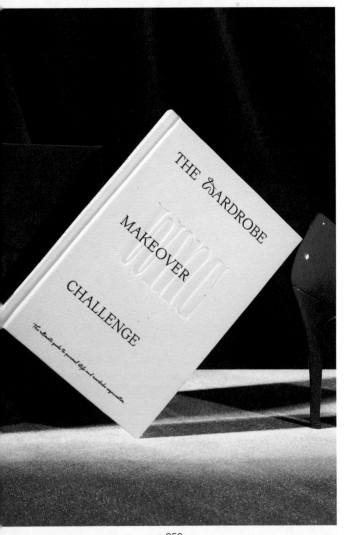

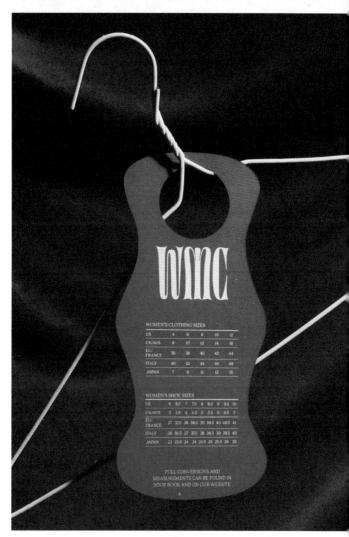

8
7
6
5
4

DEREK SWALWELL
DEREK SWALWELL
DEREK SWALWELL
DEREK SWALWELL
DEREK SWALWELL
DEREK SWALWELL
DOT COM

Introducing

DEREK SWALWELL
DEREK SWALWELL
DEREK SWALWELL
DEREK SWALWELL
DEREK SWALWELL
DEREK SWALWELL
DEREK SWALWELL

DEREK SWALWELL
DEREK SWALWELL
DEREK SWALWELL
DEREK SWALWELL
DEREK SWALWELL
DEREK SWALWELL
DOT   COM

Introducing

DEREK SWALWELL
DEREK SWALWELL
DEREK SWALWELL
DEREK SWALWELL
DEREK SWALWELL
DEREK SWALWELL
DEREK SWALWELL

DEREK SWALWELL

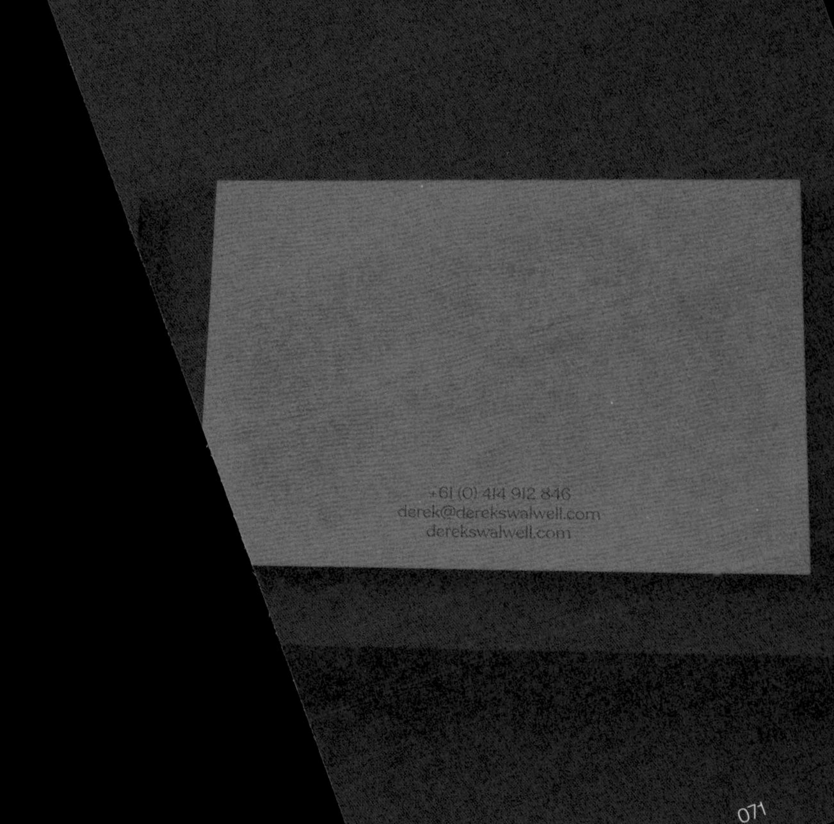

+61 (0) 414 912 846
derek@derekswalwell.com
derekswalwell.com

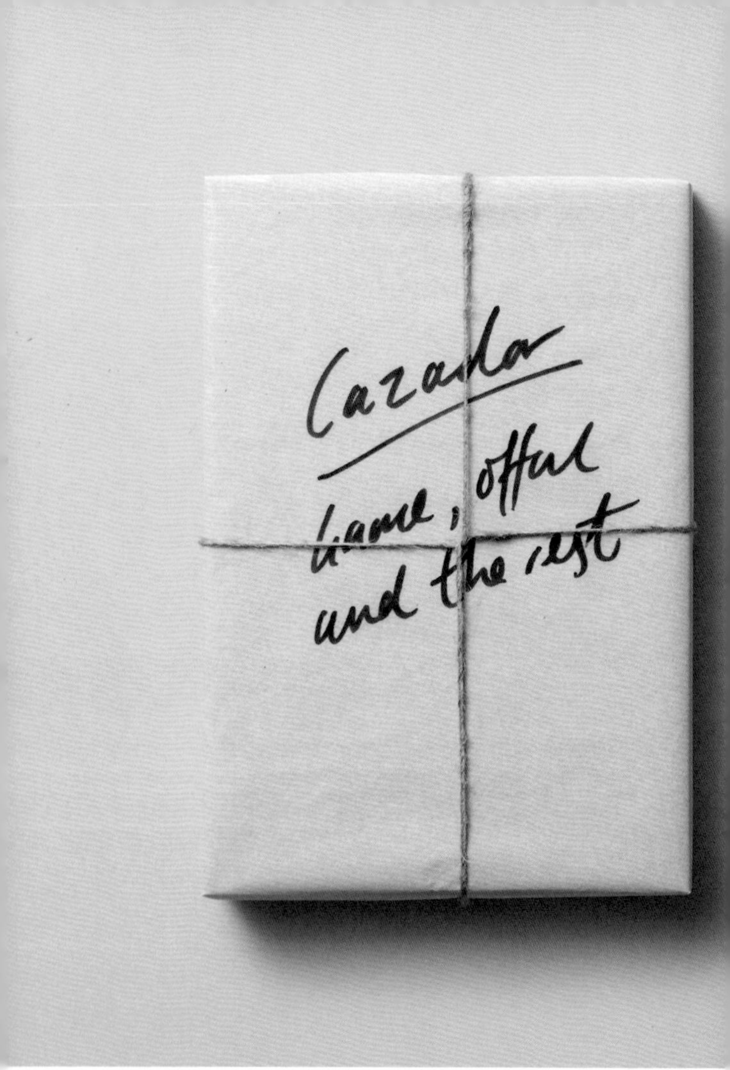
Cazador
Game, offal
and the rest

game
offal
&
the rest

Cazador

game
offal
& the rest

game
offal
&
the rest

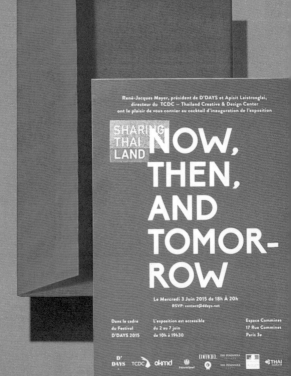

René-Jacques Mayer, président de D'DAYS et Apisit
directeur du TCDC — Thailand Creative & Desig
ont le plaisir de vous convier au cocktail d'inauguration

SHARING
THAI
LAND
NOW,
THEN

René-Jacques
directeur
ont le plaisir de vou

SHARING
THAI
LAND

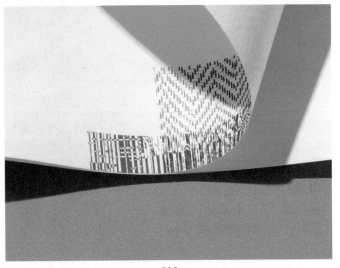

089

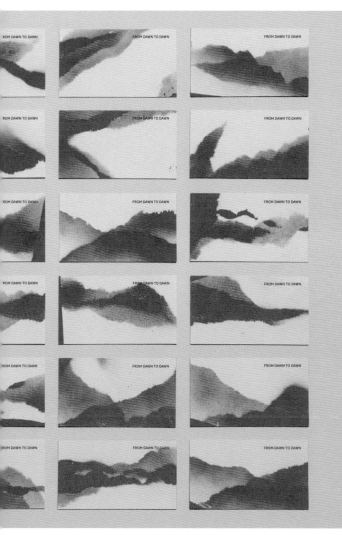

"When we want to communicate through form, we tend to use monotone. Only when form alone is not enough to convey the intended message, we use colour(s)."

이광호(1967-)

이것은 그림을 나의 촉각적 표현욕구가 가장 잘 드러나는 시리즈이다. 화폭 전반에서 마니 포함은 바느에서 떠나가기 떠올음 한다. 자리는 방망을 그리기 앞에서 바라 낡음에 자리옵하기 관적을 원치는 조재한다고 구체에 영반의 운동이상반이 사전점이 휴식점이 무대되는 두 순간에서의 그리기의 게임을 느린다.

Kwangho Lee(1967-)

My painting series of continues most explicitly reveal my desire for tactile expression. The spines of the cactus play the pivotal part in my work. These spines are the muses of my constrained scratching with needles before the paint dries out. The moment when the tactility of the cactus is emphasized as the solid and neat form of it feels is agitated by the spread it is at this very moment when I can totally exposed to the sheer pleasure of the art of painting.

3.6 TO 28.9.2015

WALKING IN THE DREAMS

潛行夢空間

康樂及文化事務署呈獻 · 香港文化博物館籌劃
Presented by the Leisure and Cultural Services Department
Organised by the Hong Kong Heritage Museum

進入十一個當代藝術家的夢空間
窺視那潛藏你內心的夢

參展藝術家 Participating Artists:
梁美萍 Joey Leung
梁淼靖 Leung Miw-ping
伍韶勁 Kingsley Ng
Ordinary Cavemen
譚偉平 Tam Wai-ping
謝瑞麟 Sara Tse
王禾璧 Adrian Wong
王永慧 Wong Chi-yung
黃琮瑜 Kacey Wong
楊嘉輝 Samson Young

Take a peek at the dreams
buried deep in your heart through
the eleven dreamy spaces
created by contemporary artists

香港文化博物館
Hong Kong Heritage Museum
1 Man Lam Road, Sha Tin, Hong Kong

開放時間 Opening Hours:
星期一、三至五上午10時至下午6時
星期六、日及公眾假期上午10時至下午7時
星期二(公眾假期除外)休館
10am–6pm on Monday, Wednesday to Friday
10am–7pm on Saturday, Sunday & public holidays
Closed on Tuesday (except public holidays)

博物館入場費 Admission (一人一票 per person):
$10 成人 (標準票價) / $7 二十人或以上團體 /
$5 全日制學生、殘疾人士 (和一名陪同照顧者) 及
六十歲或以上長者 / 四歲以下兒童免費 /
逢星期三免費
$10 Adults (Standard) /
$7 Groups of 20 persons or more /
$5 Full-time students, people with disabilities
(and one accompanying minder) and
elderly aged 60 or above /
Free admission for children aged below 4 /
Free admission on Wednesday

直達博物館門外的巴士路線
Bus routes to the museum:
A41 · 642 · 72A · 80M · 86 · 89 · 282
香港鐵路的乘客:
從車公廟站步行5分鐘線 ·
往沙田城大圍站步行15分鐘便可到達線
A 5-minute walk from Che Kung
Temple Station or a 15-minute walk
from Sha Tin or Tai Wai Station

查詢 Enquiries: (852) 2180 8188
www.heritagemuseum.gov.hk

WALKING

IN THE DREAMS

3.6 TO 28.9.2015

進入十一個當代藝術家的夢空間
窺視那潛藏你內心的夢

康樂及文化事務署主辦　香港文化博物館籌劃
Presented by the Leisure and Cultural Services Department
Organised by the Hong Kong Heritage Museum

參展藝術家 Participating Artists:
梁美萍 Joey Leung
梁美萍 Leung Mee-ping
伍韶勁 Kingsley Ng
綠腰蝶 So Yan-kei
譚偉平 Tam Wai-ping
黃麗斯 Sara Tse
王浩然 Adrian Wang
王志勇 Wong Chi-yung
黃金慧 Kacey Wong
楊嘉輝 Samson Young

Take a peek at the dreams
buried deep in your heart through
the eleven dreamy spaces
created by contemporary artists

潛行夢

間空

香港文化博物館
香港沙田文林路一號
Hong Kong Heritage Museum
1 Man Lam Road, Sha Tin, Hong Kong

開放時間 Opening Hours:
星期一、三至五上午10時至下午6時
星期六、日及公眾假期上午10時至下午7時
星期二（公眾假期除外）休館
10am-6pm on Monday, Wednesday to Friday
10am-7pm on Saturday, Sunday & public holidays
Closed on Tuesday (except public holidays)

博物館入場費 Admission (一人一票 per person):
$10 成人（標準票價）／$7 二十人或以上團體／
$5 全日制學生、殘疾人士（和一名同行的看護人）及
六十歲或以上高齡人士／四歲以下幼兒免費／
逢星期三免費
$10 Adults (Standard) /
$7 Groups of 20 persons or more /
$5 Full-time students, people with disabilities
(and one accompanying minder) and
elderly aged 60 or above /
Free admission for children aged below 4 /
Free admission on Wednesday.

直達博物館的巴士路線：
Bus routes to the museum:
A41、E42、72A、80M、86、89、282
要往博物館MTR：
從車公廟站步行約13分鐘便可到達
A 5-minute walk from Che Kung
Temple Station or a 15-minute walk
from Sha Tin or Tai Wai Station

查詢 Enquiries: (852) 2180 8188
www.heritagemuseum.gov.hk

康樂及文化事務署　文化
Leisure and Cultural Services Department

WALKING IN THE DREAMS

3.6 TO 28.9.2015

進入十一個當代藝術家的夢空間
窺視那深藏你內心的夢

康樂及文化事務署主辦 香港文化博物館籌劃
Presented by the Leisure and Cultural Services Department
Organized by the Hong Kong Heritage Museum

潛行夢
間空

參與藝術家 Participating Artists:
梁嘉賢 Josy Leung
梁美萍 Leung Mee-ping
伍韶勁 Kingsley Ng
普通人 Ordinary Cavemen
蘇晏祈 So Yan-kei
譚偉平 Tam Wai-ping
謝淑婷 Sara Tse
王志勇 Adnan Wong
王永勝 Wong Chi-yung
黃淑賢 Kacey Wong
楊嘉輝 Samson Young

Take a peek at the dreams
buried deep in your heart through
the eleven dreamy spaces
created by contemporary artists

香港文化博物館
香港沙田文林路一號
Hong Kong Heritage Museum
1 Man Lam Road, Sha Tin, Hong Kong

開放時間 Opening Hours:
星期一、三至五上午10時至下午6時
星期六、日及公眾假期上午10時至下午7時
星期二(公眾假期除外)休息
10am–6pm on Monday, Wednesday to Friday
10am–7pm on Saturday, Sunday & public holidays
Closed on Tuesday (except public holidays)

博物館入場費 Admission（一人一票 per person）:
$10 成人（標準票價）/ $7 二十人或以上團體 /
$5 全日制學生、殘疾人士（另一名陪同的看護人）及
六十歲或以上長者人士 / 四歲以下免費 / 星期三
免費開放進場

$10 Adults (Standard) /
$7 Groups of 20 persons or more /
$5 Full-time students, people with disabilities
(and one accompanying minder) and
elderly aged 60 or above /
Free admission for children aged below 4 /
Free admission on Wednesday

直達博物館門外的巴士路線
Bus routes to the museum:
A41、F40、72A、80M、86、89、282
香港城巴其他
從車公廟站步行5分鐘或
從沙田火車站步行15分鐘便可到達
A 5 minute walk from Ché Yung
Temple Station or a 15-minute walk
from Sha Tin or Tai Wai Station

查詢 Enquiries (852) 2180 8188
www.heritagemuseum.gov.hk

El Carousel

20 Carnaby Street
London, W1E 7DR
T +44 (0)20 7183 8895
E info@elcarousel.co.uk
W www.elcarousel.co.uk

Project title:
Insert project title here

Date: 00-00-00

Contents:
– File name
– File name
– File name
– File name

El Carousel

22 Carnaby Street
London, W1F 7DB
T +44 (0)20 7183 8895
E info@elcarousel.co.uk
W www.elcarousel.co.uk

Date _____

Client _____

Project _____

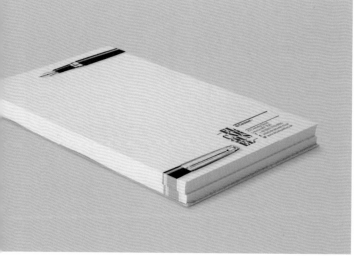

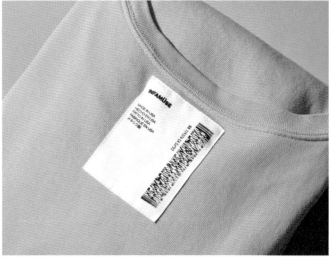

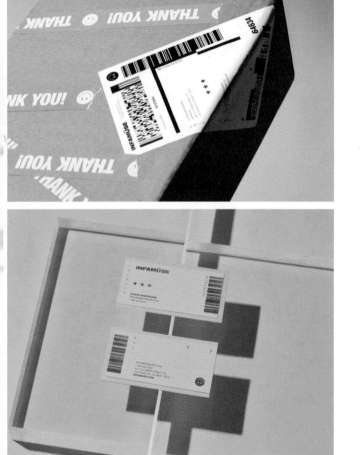

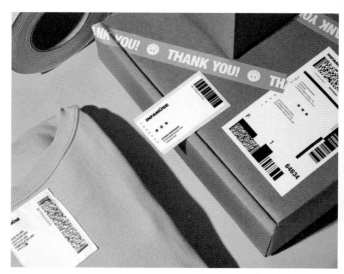

123

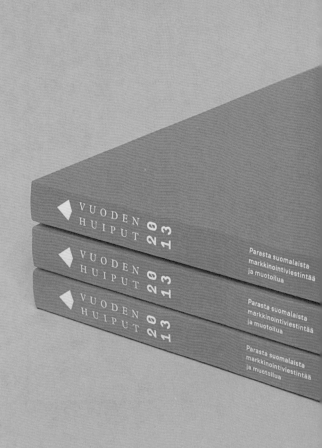

VUODEN
HUIPUT 2013

Parasta suomalaista
markkinointiviestintää
ja muotoilua

VUODEN
HUIPUT 2013

Parasta suomalaista
markkinointiviestintää
ja muotoilua

VUODEN
HUIPUT 2013

Parasta suomalaista
markkinointiviestintää
ja muotoilua

CHINESE BBQ SHOAT RIB BUNS
MISO SALMON CRISPY FRIES
GARLIC CUMIN LAMB KEBAB
DEEP FRIED VEGETABLE SPRING ROLL
SHRIMP SATAY
LEMON CHICKEN STICKS
DYNAMITE SHRIMP
BEEF SATAY
JAPANESE STYLE CHICKEN WINGS

ENTREÉ

SOY BY SATO

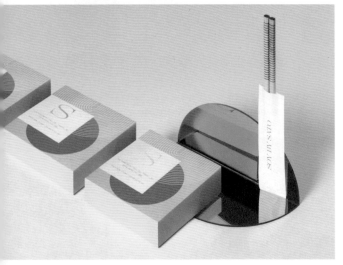

133

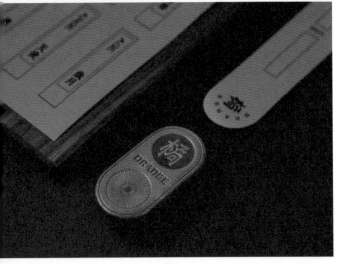

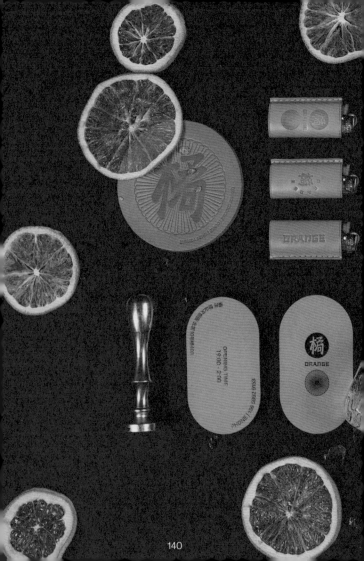

ORANGE

ORANGE 橘子	ON 檸檬	ORE 礦石	OR 戒許
ONE 唯一	OG 老炮	ORANG	RANG
RAGE	RAN	天使	盧月

PHONE

NAME

ORANGE

橘 ORANGE

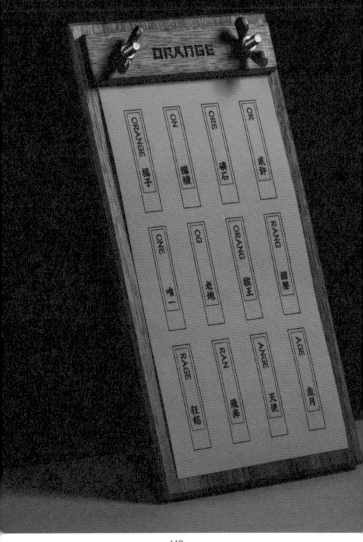

142

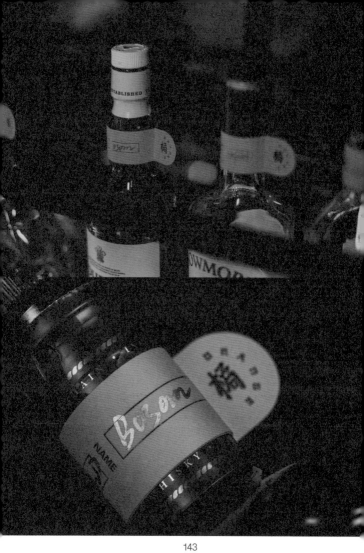

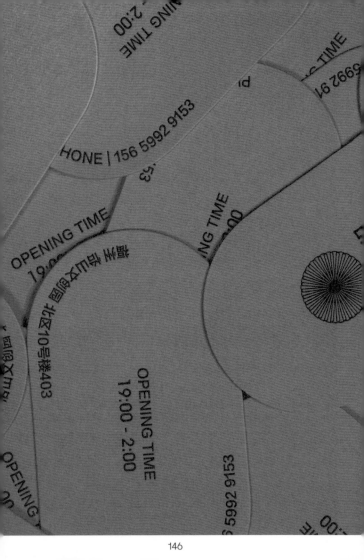

OPENING TIME 2:00

PHONE | 156 5992 9153

53

OPENING TIME
19:00

NG TIME
00

NG TIME
00

北区10号楼403

OPENING TIME
19:00 - 2:00

6 5992 9153

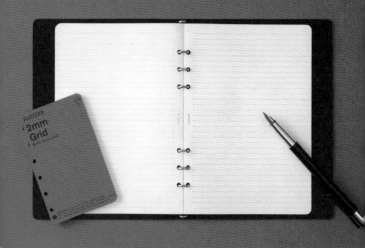

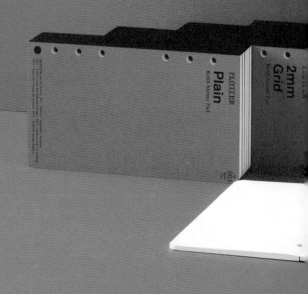

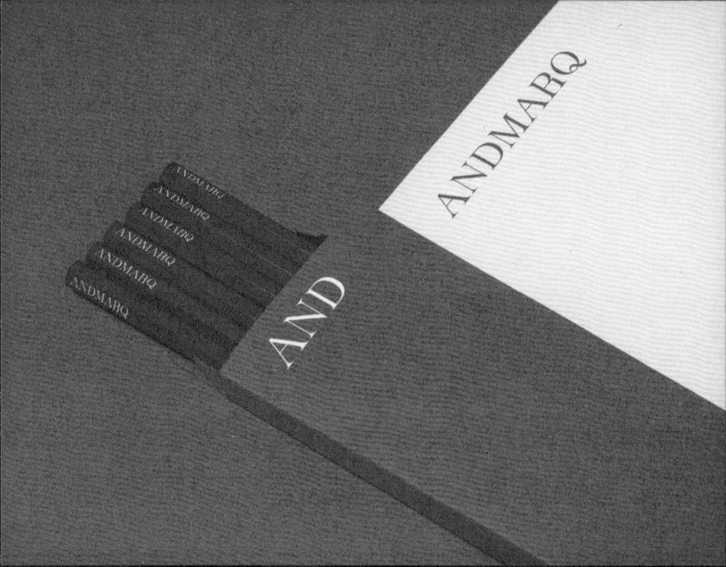
ANDMARQ
AND
ANDMARQ

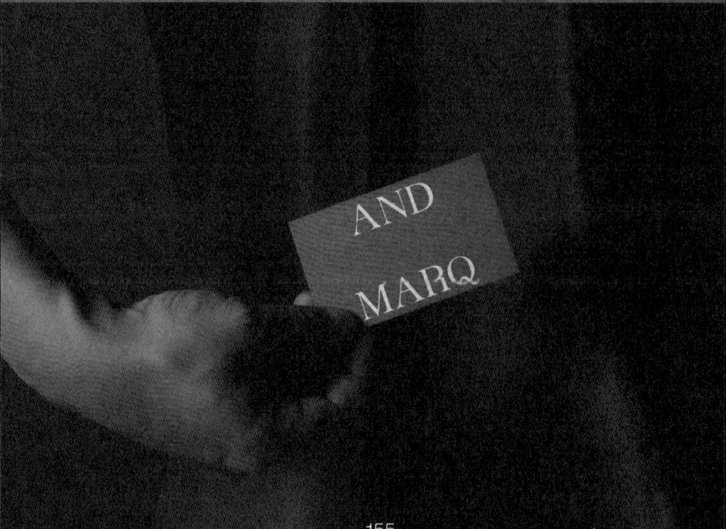
AND
MARQ

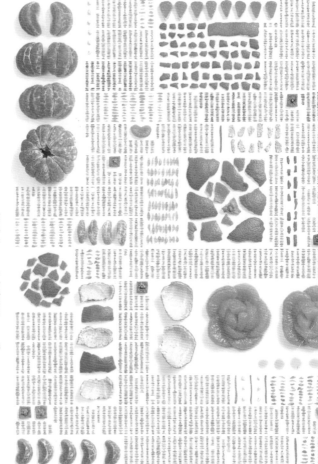

世界のことを、静岡なりに。

静岡新聞
📞0120-89-4311

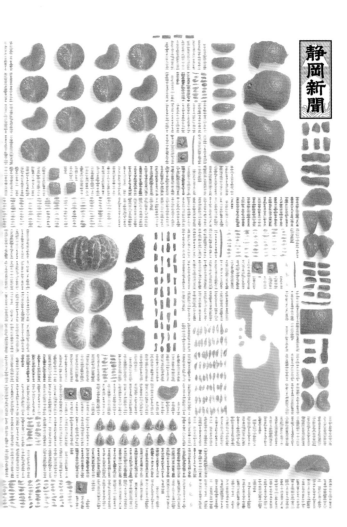

静岡新聞

167

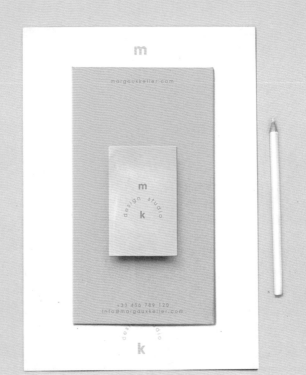

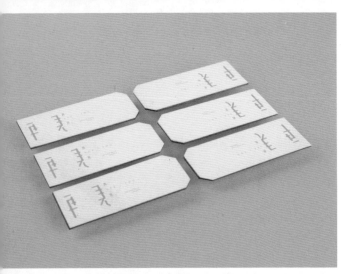

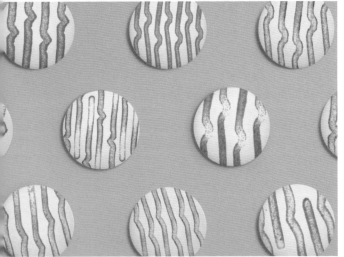

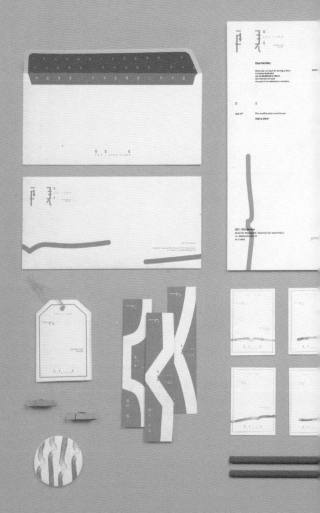

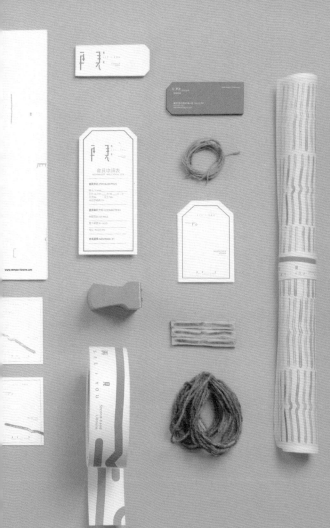

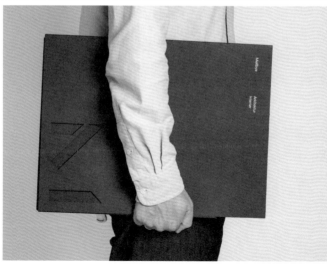

TWO
THOU
SAND
FIF
TEEN

HAND
MADE
&
PRINTED
IN THE
USA

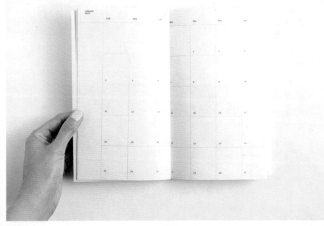

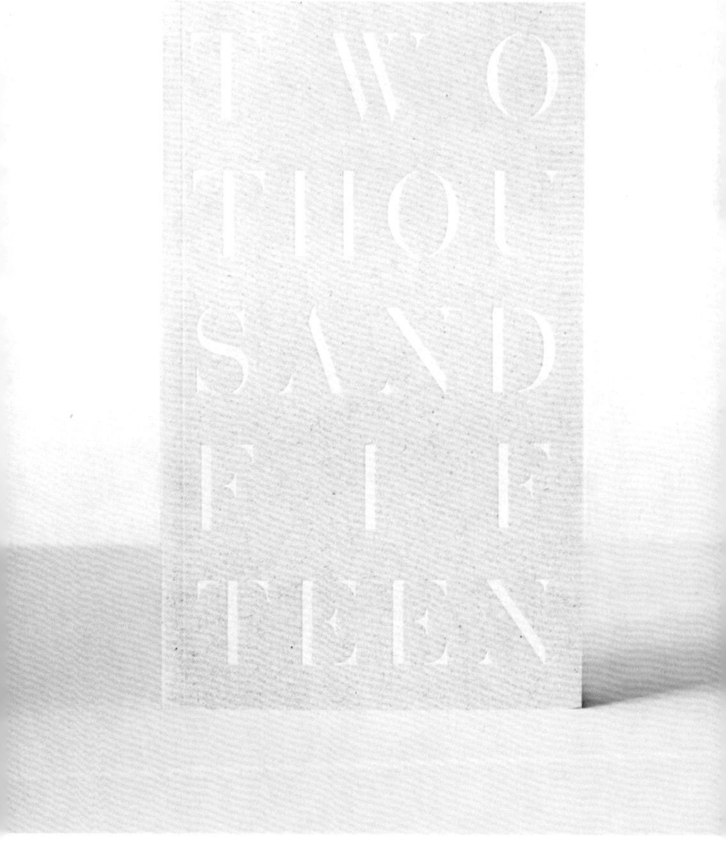

TWO
THOU
SAND
FIF
TEEN

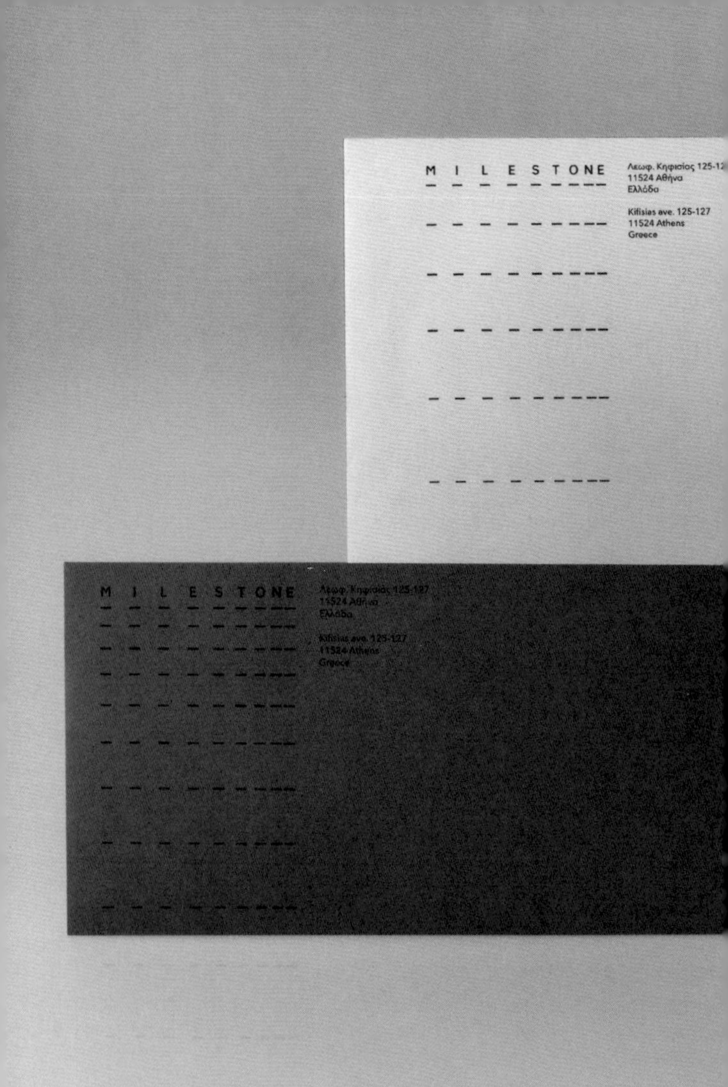
M I L E S T O N E
Λεωφ. Κηφισίας 125-12
11524 Αθήνα
Ελλάδα
Kifisias ave. 125-127
11524 Athens
Greece
M I L E S T O N E

E S T O N E   Public affairs &
                 strategic
                 communication

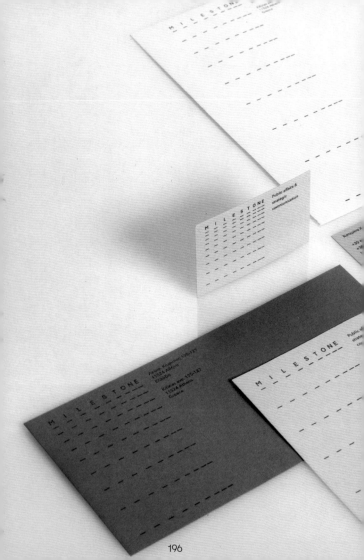

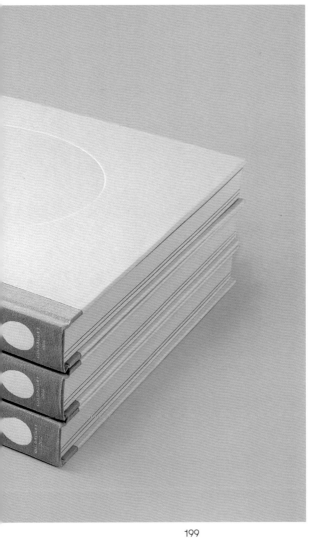

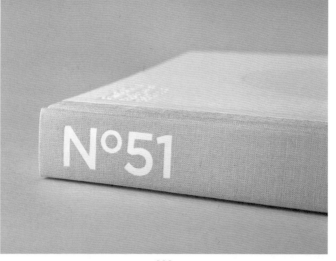

"The subtle design details monotone produces appeal to us on a more tactile level and offer us physical proof of an idea."

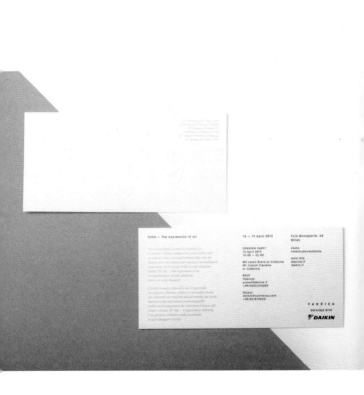

FUHA — The expression of air

14 — 19 April 2015

Foro Bonaparte, 60
Milan

OPENING PARTY
16 April 2015
18:00 — 22:00

#fuha
#fabbricalovesdaikin

M2 Lanza Brera or Cadorna
M1 Cairoli Castello
or Cadorna

who info
fabrica.it
daikin.it

RSVP
Fabrica
press@fabrica.it
+39/0422/516209

Daikin
daikin@usmedia.com
+39/02/8130561

FABRICA

BREATHES WITH

⚡DAIKIN

205

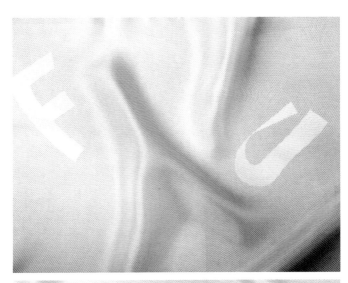

FUHA
The expression of air

SALONE DEL MOBILE
14 — 19 APRIL 2015

Foro Bonaparte, 60
Milan

#fuha
#fabricalovesdaikin

fuha.info
fabrica.it
daikin.it

FABRICA

BREATHES WITH

DAIKIN

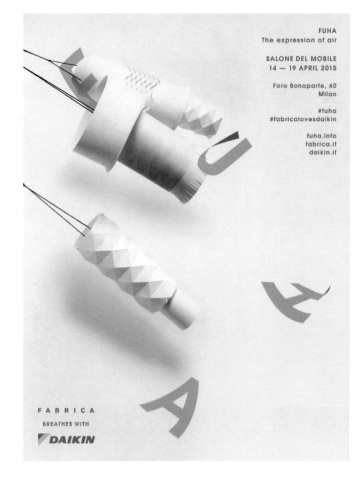

FUHA
The expression of air

SALONE DEL MOBILE
14 — 19 APRIL 2015

Foro Bonaparte, 60
Milan

#fuha
#fabricalovesdaikin

fuha.info
fabrica.it
daikin.it

FABRICA

BREATHES WITH

DAIKIN

224

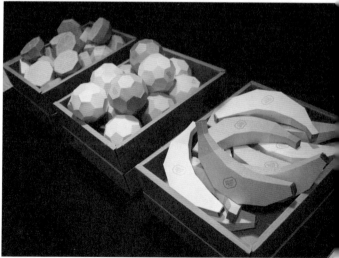

229

FISCO ✪ | 600mm/24in
L3-060 Made in the EU

Extra Heavy Duty | Professional Level

237

Installations
  Kunstlerhaus Dortmund,
  Germany

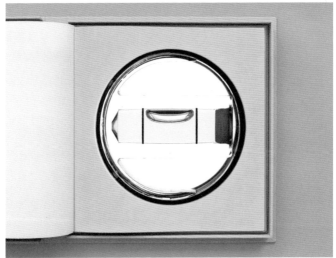

"We wanted to reference bees without being too literal. So, yellow and black made a lot of sense."

BESPACE
BESPAC
Dear Malala,
Lorem ipsum dolor sit amet, consetetuer adipiscing elit, sed diam nonum
my nibh euismod tincidunt ut laoreet dolore magna aliquam erat
Uwisi enim ad minim veniam, quis nostrud exerci tatesfion
suscipit lobortis nisl ut aliquip ex ea commodo consequat. Duis
eum iriure dolor in hendrerit in vulputate velit esse molestie
illum dolore eu feugiat nulla facilisis at vero eros et accumsan
dignissim qui blandit praesent luptatum zzril delenit augue
feugait nulla facilisi. Nam liber tempor cum soluta nobis
congue nihil imperdiet doming id quod mazim placerat
Typi non habent claritatem insitam; est usus legentis
claritatem. Investigationes demonstraverunt lectores
legunt saepius. Claritas est etiam processus
mutationem uetudium lectorum. Mirum est
quam nunc putamus parum claram,
per seacula quarta decima et quinta
nobis videntur parum clari, fiant
Warm regards,
Founder

...rawl. But by all means, keep moving. **Martin Luther King Jr.**

Our turn, now.
To work for the wealth of good.
To spark and stoke the audacious.
To profit the world.

The challenge is great. But the challenges are greater still. For excellence, guided by enigmas and creatively transformed into enterprise, ensures that positive social action becomes lasting global impact.

So at this moment, it's our turn to give flight to this next generation of change-makers.

In our resolve time, collective wisdom is shared, honest and newly improvised. Our resolve, a new generation of twin myths & complex ingenuance, are guided & supported by the greatest thinkers & innovators in new reality, creativity, technology, philanthropy and coinage.

A true partnership that helps build strong and enduring organisations, bold new models of how to practise charity, advance social change, mobilise relief and accelerate recovery, empower economic independence, protect the environment or advocate for justice.

An organisation that can move from precept to concrete outcome—a wish for wishes becomes a well-on months rather than years.

Evolution happens daily. So with every new insight and communications too, the speed, scale and success of positive change pieces improved. And further multiplied.

Then, act act of generosity can boost the world, and interest too, the proof of its power is made evident. The sum of this single aim is shared outward, in local communities & across distant borders, creating a summer bond of compassion and humanity. Devoting all of us, inspiring us.

To see giving as a new of living.

To understand that genuine commitment produces the greatest impact.

To profit the world. Your turn, now.

BE SPACE

bespace.com

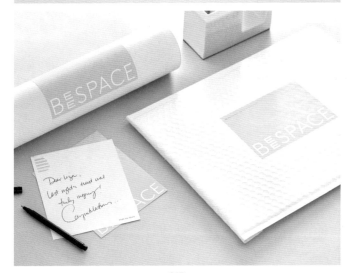

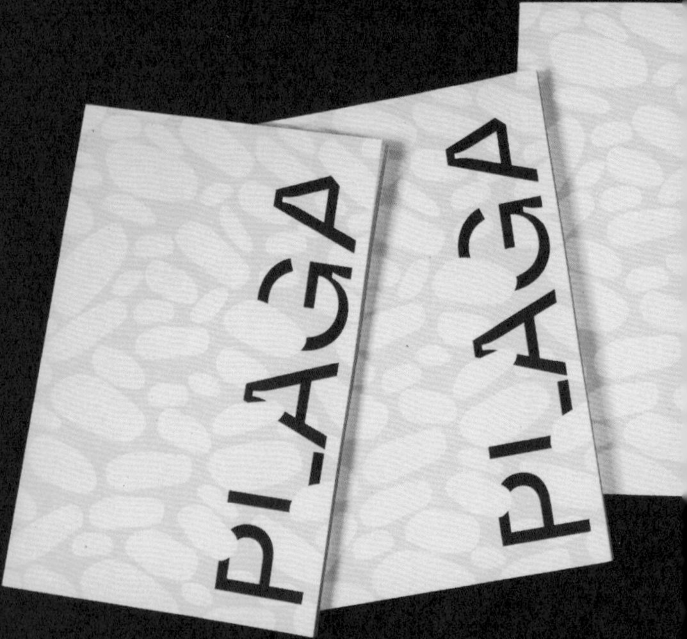
PLAGA
PLAGA

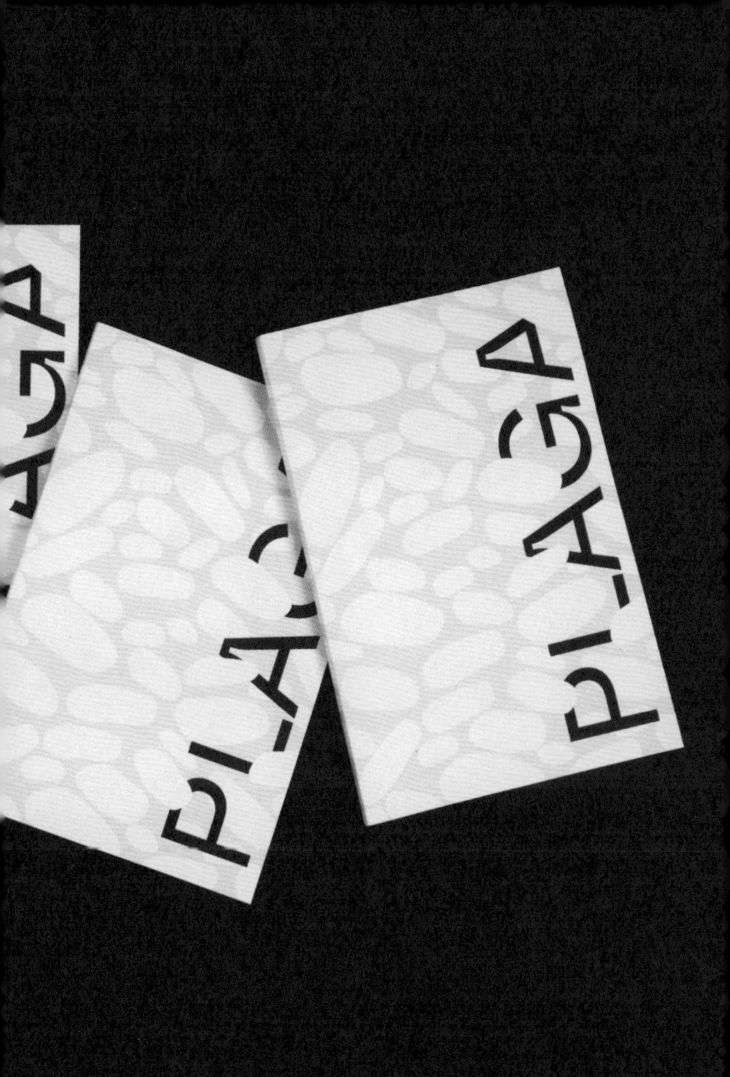

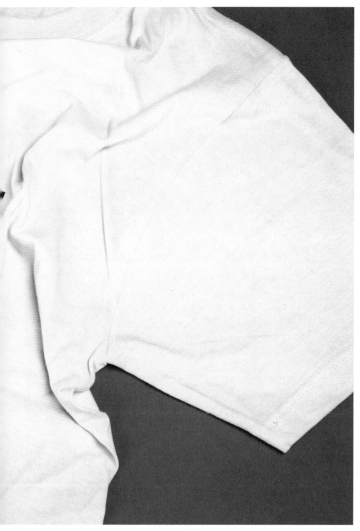

257

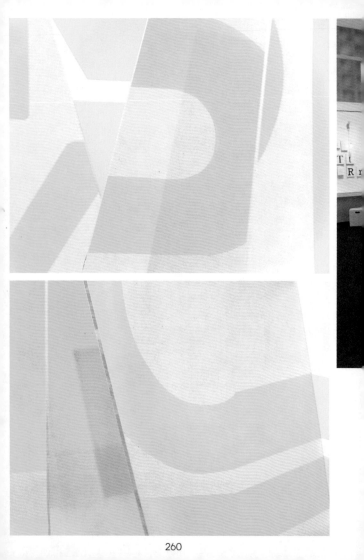

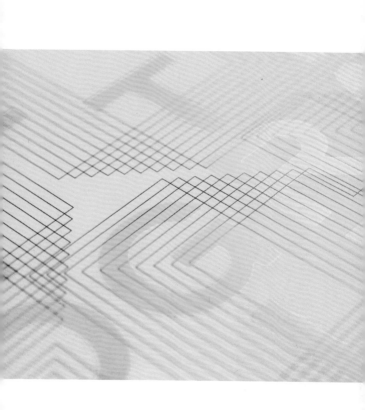

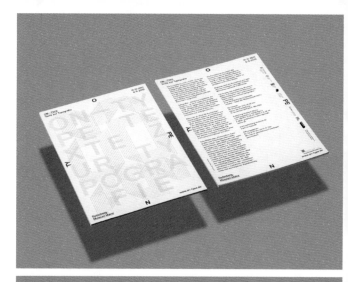

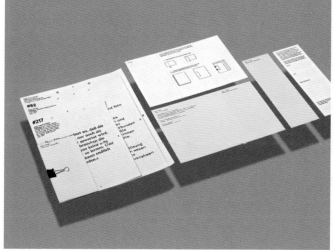

House of Photography
is a project about
forgotten memories.
In our fast living, instant
and sometimes even
disposable digital culture,
HOP aims to bring back
the charm and feeling
of anticipation in analogue
photography – elements
that are very much
missing in an age where
images are created
instantaneously by the
click of a button.

House of Photography
is a project about
forgotten memories.
In our fast living, instant
and sometimes even
disposable digital culture,
HOP aims to bring back
the charm and feeling
of anticipation in analogue
photography – elements
that are very much
missing in an age where
images are created
instantaneously by the
click of a button.

Situated in a 20-foot
container, HOP will travel
around Singapore from
October 2012 for a period
of 2 years.

HOUSE OF PHOTOGRAPHY

HOUSE OF PHOTOGRAPHY

HOP

05 Oct 2012 – 22 Oct 2013
National Library
The Plaza

24 Oct 2012 – 26 Nov 2013
Jurong
Regional Library

29 Nov 2012 – 06 Jan 2013
Yew Tee Point

HOUSE OF PHOTOGRAPHY

House of Photography is a project about forgotten memories. In our fast-living, instant and sometimes even disposable digital culture, HOP aims to bring back the charm and feeling of anticipation in analogue photography – elements that are very much missing in an age where images are created instantaneously by the click of a button.

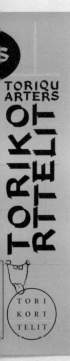

"This makes design easier when you have limited tools. It also keeps the different implementations in line with each other."

285

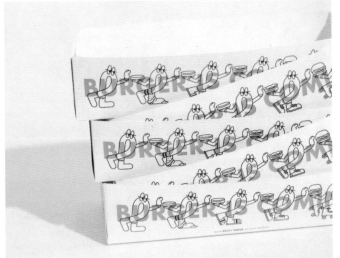

288

CLOSE YOUR EYES
FOR DRUNK

BURGER DAYS

ON BEHALF OF
LAZINESS

LAZZY BURGER
BURGER SUPPLY CO.

BURGER DAYS

LAY
ON
ME

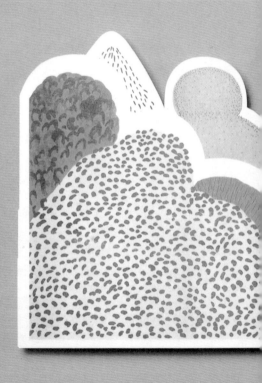

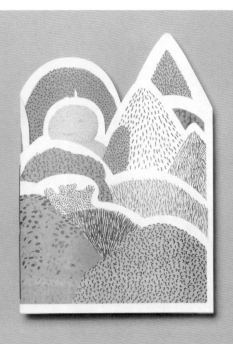

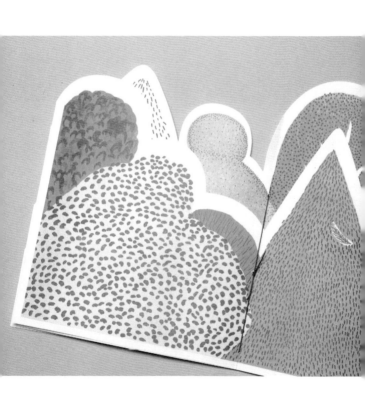

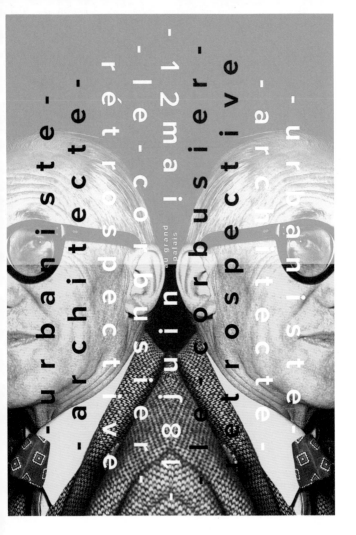

-urbaniste-
-architecte-
-le corbusier-
rétrospective-
-12 mai ... 18 août -
le grand palais

SUPER

Sugar-free
Ultra Nutritious
Purely Organic
Energy Booster
Rich Antioxidants

SUPER MATCHA

SUPER HERO OF TEAS

SUPER MATCHA™
SUPER NATURAL ENERGY BOOSTER
SUPER
슈퍼 말차
SUGAR-FREE SWEET MATCHA / 500g

RESTAURANT
SOUBOIS

1106 De Maisonneuve Ouest, Montréal   514 564 5672
Guillaume Daly - Chef Exécutif   514 805 4627
guillaume@soubois.com

La
Clef
D'Or

31
12 15

RESTAURANT
SOUBOIS

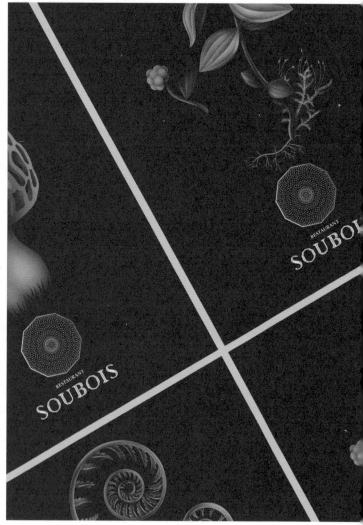

Kernit Display

"YOU MEAN A
BORN DEER AIN'T
DE GIFT DEER
OF OUR DEER,
A SH DEAR,
DAT YOU AH DE
BORN TO DE
AIN'T DE BORN?
BORN? BORN!"

316

323

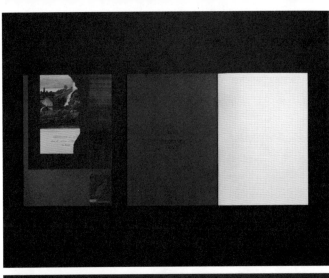

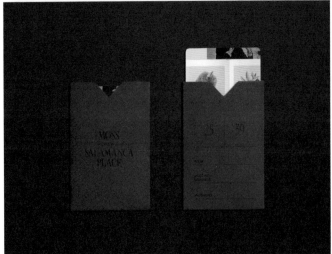

to be yourself everyday.

MADE IN JAPAN QUALITY.

NAGI_OFFICIAL_JP NAGI_OFFICIALJP

ISBN 978-9-415-5647b-f

USA

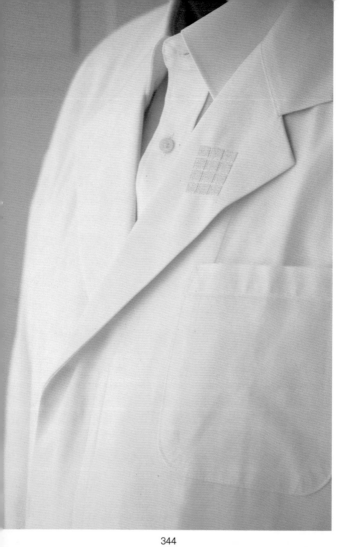

"Using mint green as the primary colour essentially gives the clinic a fresh impression and an unique atmosphere."

住吉堂鍼灸院

SUMIYOSHIDO
KAMPO LOUNGE

ICEB

2013

SANTA V

LIVE — LO

SUM

RGS

4

TTORIA

BONDI

MER

ICEBERGS
SUNDAY
BRUNCH

10AM
- 12PM

EVERY
SUNDAY

FIRST
DAY OF
SUMMER
PARTY
MONDAY
FIRST
DECEMBER

ICEBERGS
DINING ROOM AND BAR
FROM 7.30PM

RSVP Essential – events@idrb.com

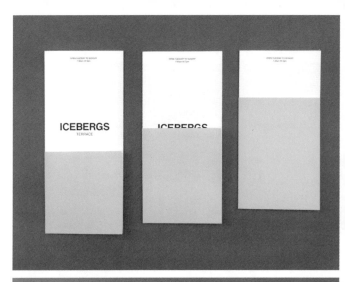

365

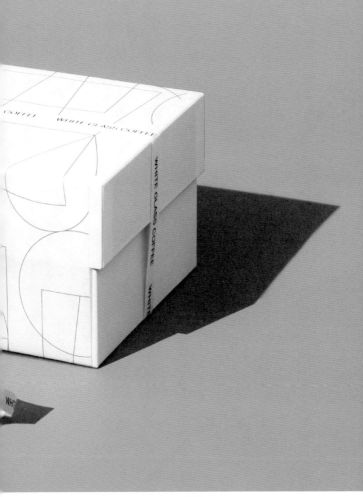

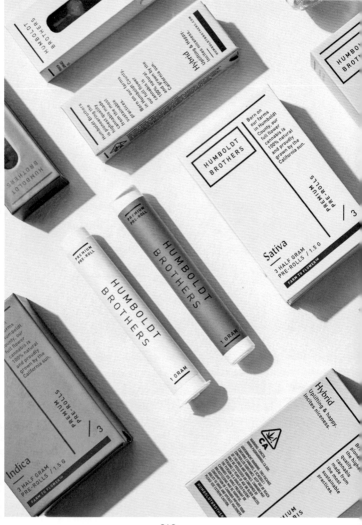

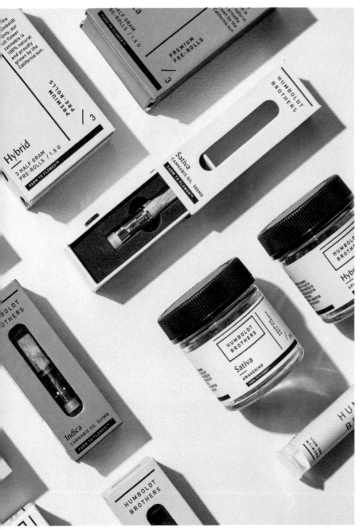

370

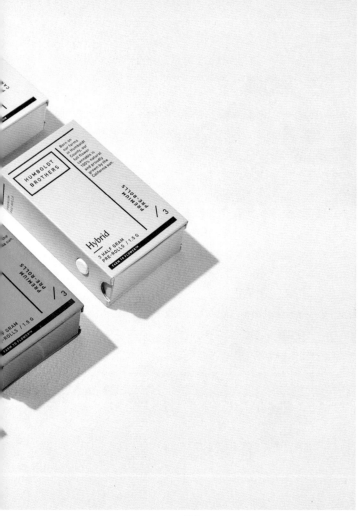

375

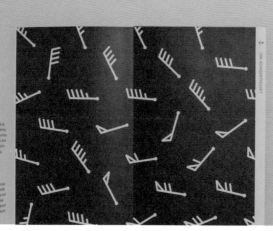

SMARAGD   HAVYARD

ROLLS-ROYCE   MØRETRYG

                           VARD   OPUS   KVALSKJÆR

Her er det svake og det sterke. Her er det høglydte og det lågmælte,
det dramatiske og det fredfulle. Her er dei store opplevingane og dei
strevsame kvardagane. Her er dei mektige kontrastane og dei fine
nyansane. Yist i havgapet, inspirert av havet og musikken.
Ein levande stad i evig endring.

MS ARCTIC
SWAN

MODECA

FOKUS
REGNSKAP

REMØY MANAGEMENT   REMØY SHIPPING

NORDEA   HERØY KOMMUNE

                    LEINEFISK

EROS

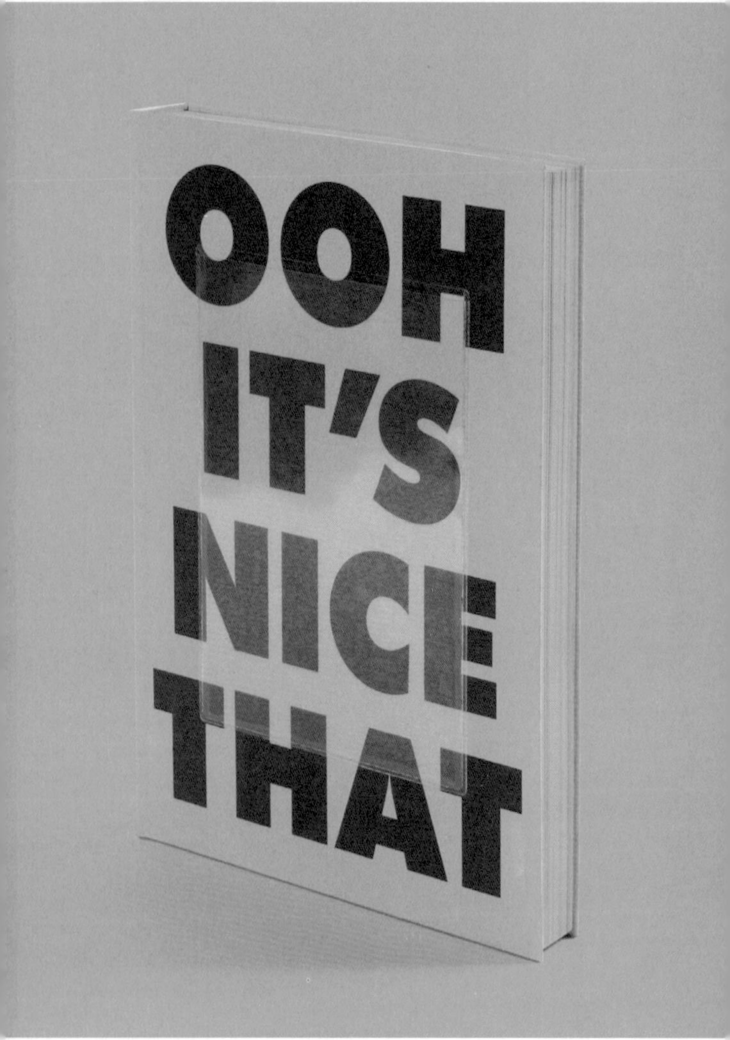
OOH
IT'S
NICE
THAT

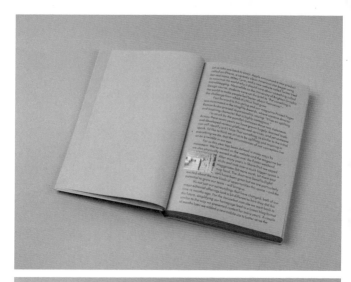

"The use of different shades of one colour helps people focus on the small differences. It feels like different colours, but because they are monotone they will always be in harmony."

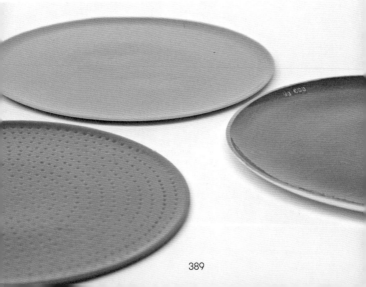

The view from Lucania is an independent organization founded by Stefano Tripodi in 2010. We support South of Italy through the implementation of audiovisual concepts, exhibitions, events, workshops, productions related to photography and cinema, overseen by international photographers and directors.

theviewfromlucania.com

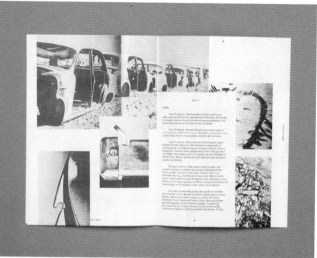

Giulia

Casa Prudenza. Faremo andare a via da questa casa, dalla Urgente di Raisi può rappresentarsi fanciullo, dal subito
col doppio motivo che ha porteria od poster gigantesco, da
questa fibrina che mi fa vedere tutto amabile.

Casa Prudenza. Rimparai faremo da quinto musica a
tutti mio aria, della natura quasi, del subito, dal quinto sesto
subito d'aula che mi si accostellano, cerenfe alle dormire.

Casa Prudenza. Nella settimana di fortepiano cogito
trumont torneà, disposizioni alle domande imbarazzanti di
realti longché caso Mepludrobeye. Guardami Giulia, quindi mi
molquisto. Il mio sia avere giorgimagio buchetti, disegni poeni
con Walter. Non ricevo avere un camello con una Cavaliere di
Mafia di mio. Bonbon, prodotto e Nilli Narti di nessi all'acero e
giorbare ca chilosse.

Mausee melendro. Non dormivi nel tuo latte, non
sostenti al sasso la camplate che sarecchi alla festa di San-
Patrizi e prendo evropro i mittri amai. Sorcani alto sono
che belle caso tua, che dimora che tua io mio. Ma la stoch di
nitico, riaberra alla mia sulla terrazza di casa. Rilevanri con ti
faretro, con il quiprengono che Maria e la ingiorno Maccio sul
Giorbar/ogni sette ambasi, suddhi, vierre la montaggio.

Una volta farenti alla giosice del cavalli mi nel asmo
che mi farevè calore. Sevelmi una Persini dinascido e Pumare
Ciladon, Maria siono fotte superno tu, dicare che stavar
allamigde. Il purti practitre il meno, di cui che era perfetto
per darlo segvetto, tutto in fonda al poloto. Ti pastia giù
non doriamo al sceleta il mio pre calvario in foncando.
Il astaruno sopra un trattore a dessoremo la mera. Ti disse

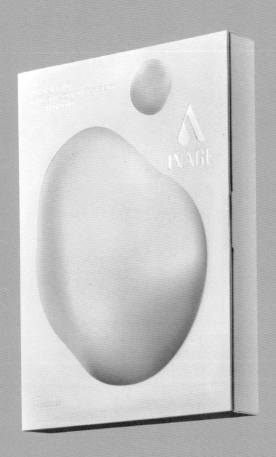

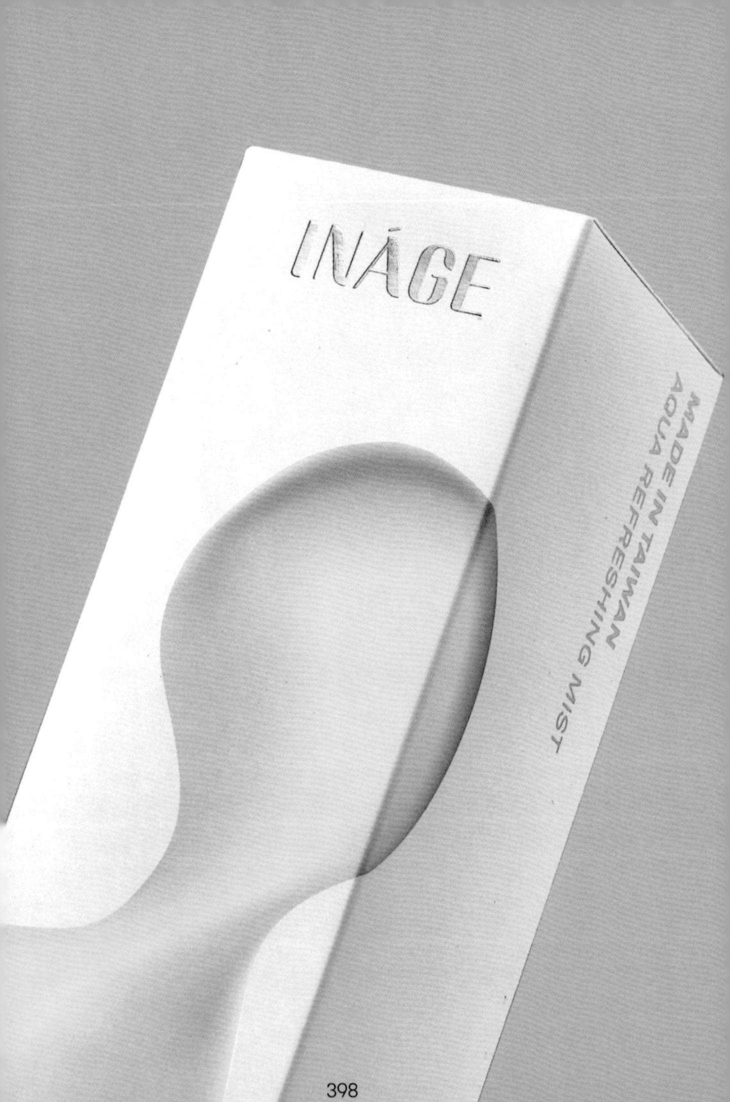
INÁGE
MADE IN TAIWAN
AQUA REFRESHING MIST

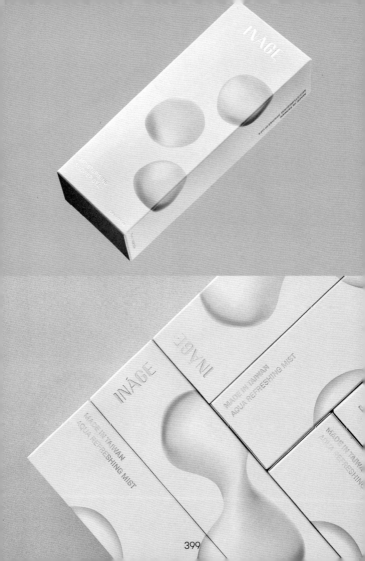

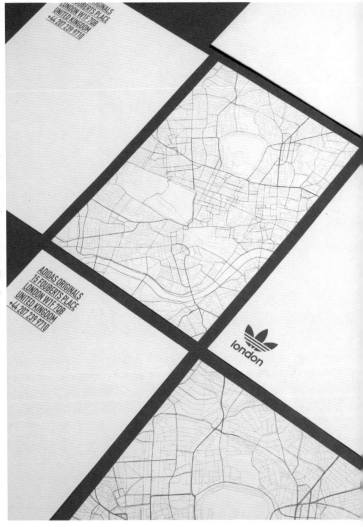

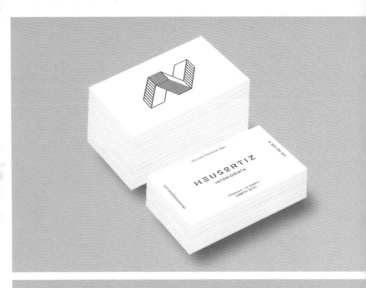

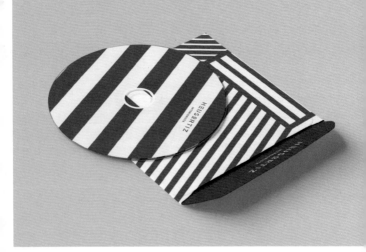

neusortiz@gmail.com

NEUSORTIZ
INTERIORISTA

or Fleming 4bis

SORTIZ
ERIORISTA

ova i la Geltrú
8800 BCN

or Fleming 4bis

SORTIZ
ERIORISTA

ova i la Geltrú
8800 BCN

M. 699 296 464

M. 699 296 464

M. 699 296

Doctor Fleming 4
Vilanova i la Gelt
08800 BCN

ツツウラウラから、いらっじゃい。このメンバーが幕張に集まる今日は、ただ一度だけ。恋してるヤツ、ヘコんでるヤツ、悩みも抱えているPOCARI SWEAT だろう。はじめましてさようなら。音楽にどうもサンキュー。歌って飲んで笑って泣くかも、ひとつよろしく。熱中したら、対策ポカリ。

夏フェスでの熱中症にはご用心。カンカン照りも雨が降っても。

どうやっても伝説のフェスになっちゃう。ぼくらがいるから。

熱中したら
対策ポカリ

POCARI SWEAT

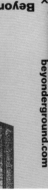

May 2014

05.05 —
06.06

city expos
street art
museums
galleries

May 2014

05.05 —
06.06

city expos
street art
museums
galleries

09.05 —
10.05

indoor festival
after party

round a festival of
graphic joy and
creativity

BEYØNDERGRØUND

Beyonderground
Helsinki

a fes
grap
crea

BEYØ
NDER
GRØU
ND

09.05 —
10.05

indoor festival
after party

05.05 —
06.06

city expos
street art
museums
galleries

a festival of
graphic joy and
creativity

Beyonderground
Helsinki

beyonderground.com

05.05 –
06.06

city expos
street art
museums
galleries

beyonderground.com

**Beyonderground
Helsinki**

a festival of
graphic joy and
creativity

Bleu Royal

Couleur 100% naturelle
100% natural colour

Gin floral distingué
Floral distinguish gin

40% alc./vol.
70 cl

Bleu
Royal
Gin bleu floral
Floral blue gin
Produit du
Québec, Canada
12 x 750 ml
07/16/2018

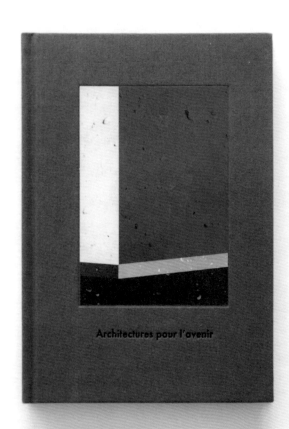

Architectures pour l'avenir

Architectures pour l'avenir exposition du 16 février au 23 mars. Ouvert tous les jours sauf lundis, mardis et jours fériés, de 13h à 18h. Les vendredis, ouverture en nocturne, uniquement de 15h à 20h. Entrée libre

Autour de l'exposition
À la villa Noailles

Conférence « Architectures pour l'avenir »
avec Vincent Parreira (AAVP Architecture),
Luca Galofaro et Carmelo Baglivo (IaN+),
dimanche 16 février à 10h30, sur réservation

Signature du catalogue par les architectes
présentés dans l'exposition dimanche 16 février
à 14h30

Atelier en famille avec Vincent Parreira,
architecte, dimanche 23 février de 15h à 18h
sur réservation

Visite commentée de l'exposition
- par Florence Sarano, dimanche 2 mars à 15h
- par un médiateur tous les samedis à 11h
jusqu'au 22 mars
- par un médiateur mercredi 26 février
et mercredi 5 mars à 15h pour les enfants
de 8 à 11 ans et à 16h pour les enfants
de 12 à 16 ans.

Rencontre « Expériences pour l'avenir »*
par Vincent Parreira
*accessible exclusivement aux acteurs
de l'éducation (écoles, associations...)
mercredi 19 mars à 10h

Visites pour les groupes scolaires
pendant la durée de l'exposition, accompagné
d'un médiateur. Réservation par email auprès
des médiateurs.

Hors les murs

Conférences de Vincent Parreira
à l'école d'architecure de Marseille
lundi 24 février à 19h, mardi 18 mars
à 19h

**Petit château Saint-Pierre,
dit villa Gandarillas**

Visites du chantier du futur atelier de
prototypage pour la mode et le design,
commentée par un médiateur, chaque
samedi jusqu'au 22 mars, départ à 10h
de la villa Noailles, sur inscription

Présentation du projet de rénovation
de la villa Gandarillas par Loïc Julienne,
architecte, agence Construire
mercredi 5 mars à 18h - villa Noailles

Médiateurs
Hélène Fontaine :
h.fontaine@villanoailles-hyeres.com
Guillaume Vacquier :
g.vacquier@villanoailles-hyeres.com
T : +33 (0)4 98 08 01 95

Tous les évènements programmés
par la villa Noailles sont
gratuits et accessibles à tous
dans la limite des places disponibles.

villa Noailles, communauté d'agglomération
Toulon Provence Méditerranée
Montée Noailles · 83400 Hyères
T : +33 (0)4 98 08 01 98
www.villanoailles-hyeres.com

437

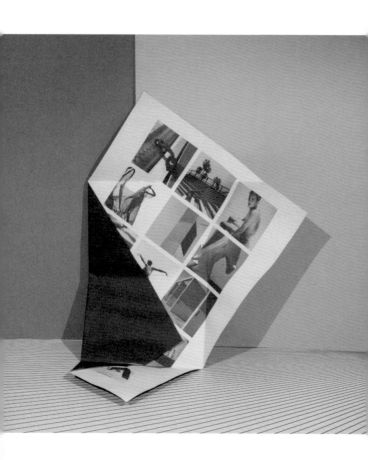

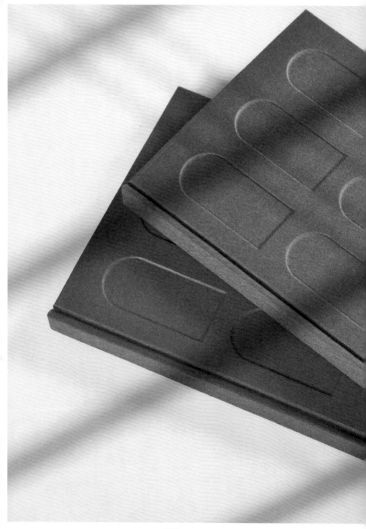

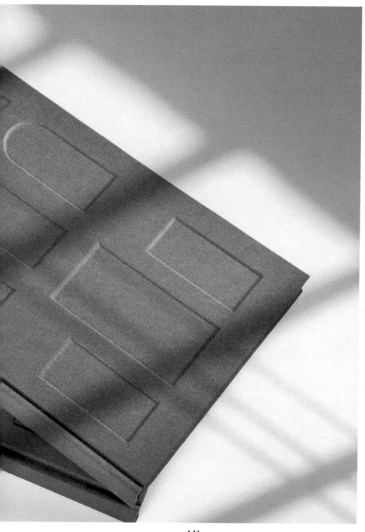

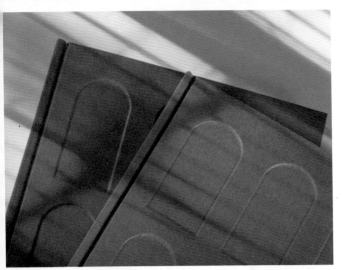

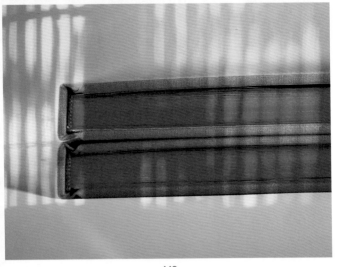

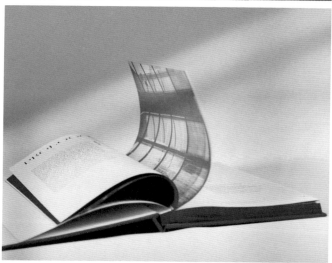

Fondazione
Guggenheim

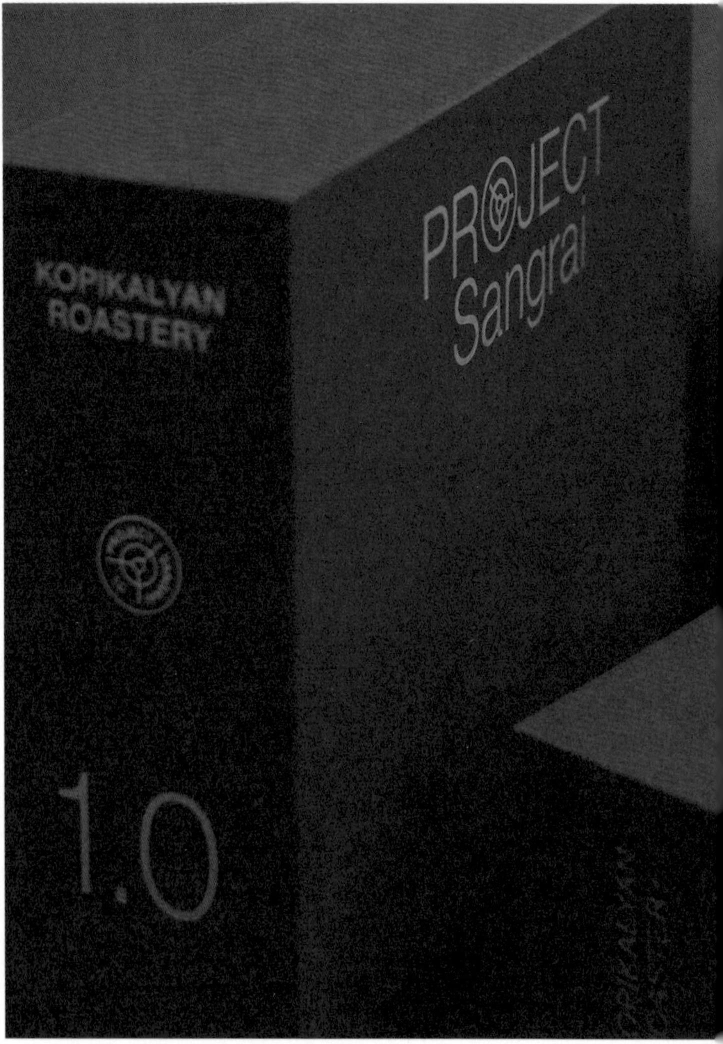
KOPIKALYAN
ROASTERY
1.0
PROJECT
Sangrai

449

PROJECT
Sangrai 1.0

kopikalyan

Sebuah project untuk menjadikan ruang sangrai Kopikalyan wadah bagi orang-orang inspiratif berkolaborasi memperkenalkan kopi Indonesia ke pasar yang lebih luas dengan caranya masing-masing. Kopikalyan Roastery menampilkan kopi Indonesia yang spesial dikurasi dengan mengikuti tema yang berbeda di setiap koleksinya.

Project Sangrai 1.0 berjudul SOSOK KALYAN. Setiap bulannya, satu figur perkopian Indonesia akan mampir ke ruang sangrai Kopikalyan, mengkurasi dua kopi berkualitas Indonesia untuk bisa dinikmati kalyan selama sebulan penuh.

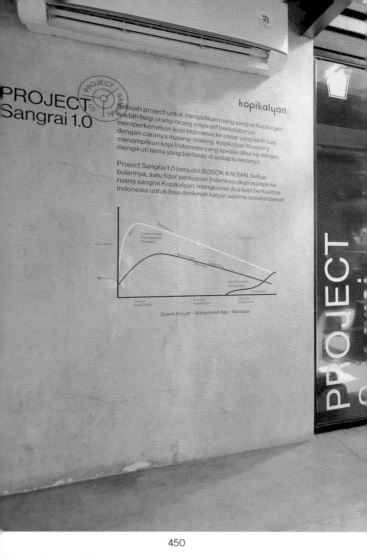

Sosok Kalyan - Muhammad Aga - Manbaya

PROJECT
Sangrai 1.0

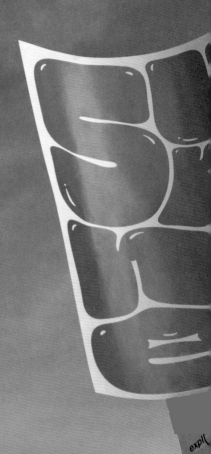

expl(

ABOUT THE ARTIST

Ranging from absurd inflatable suits to architectural subversions, Jimmy Bastard's inflated artworks engage his audiences with a playful sense of the unexpected. "I try to find the line between the spectacle and the absurd," he says. "If I can make something the eye can't quite put in a category, then maybe there's going to be a truer circuit and you'll have a genuine interaction."

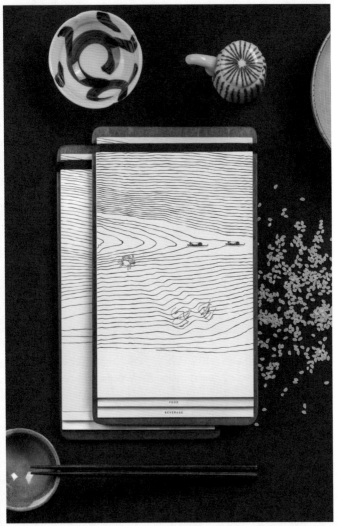

FOOD

BEVERAGE

465

"With a biro pen, there is always a possibility to go deeper into the depths of blue by adding and crossing more and more lines."

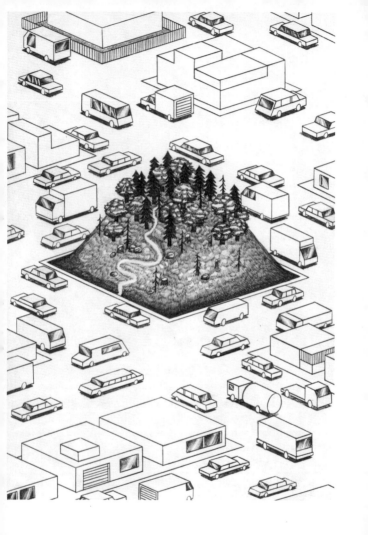

474

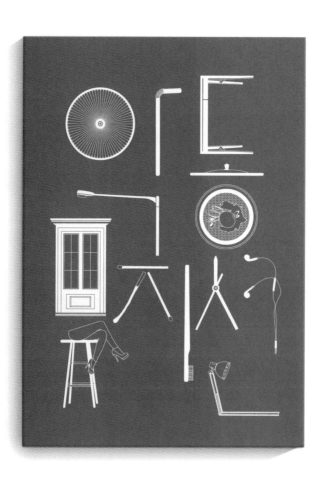

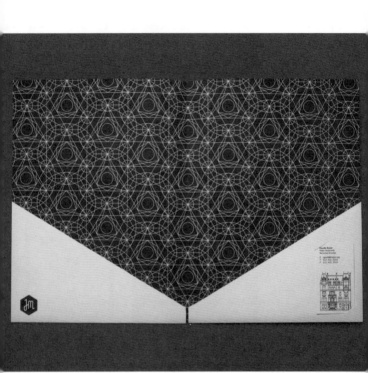

481

MAFALDINE
cook 9 min

JAZZ PASTA

facts

	126
	14G
	2G
	69,7G
	3G
	5MG
	10%
	10%
	2%
	8%

eat flour, water

Jazz is a music genre that originated in the African-American communities of New Orleans, United States. It originated in the late 19th and early 20th centuries, and developed from roots in blues and ragtime. Jazz is seen by many as 'America's classical music'. Since the 1920s Jazz Age, jazz has become recognized as a major form of musical expression. It then emerged in the form of independent traditional and popular musical styles, all linked by the common bonds of African-American and European-American musical parentage with a performance orientation. Jazz is characterized by swing and blue notes, call and response vocals, polyrhythms and improvisation. Intellectuals around the world have hailed jazz as 'one of America's original art forms'.

JAZZ

ADD PESTO!

484

AFALDINE
cook 9 min

ASTA

500G

OPEN HERE

INGREDIENTS:
semolina (wheat),
durum wheat flour.

VITAMINS/MINERALS:
vitamin b3 (niacin), iron
(ferrous sulfate), vitamin b1
(thiamine mononitrate),
vitamin b2 (riboflavin), folic
acid.

Contains wheat ingredients.
This product is
manufactured
on equipment that processes
products containing eggs.

PAP PP

MAFA
COO

JAZZ PA

HOW TO COOK:

1 Bring a pan of water
and season it with salt

2. Add the spaghetti
gently until all the stra
beneath the water lev
again to make sure the
stuck together.

3. Cook following the p
instructions to receive
"Al-dente" result.

9 min

4. Check the pasta whe
is up by biting into a st
should be cooked thro
firm. Cook for a furthe
you need to, or if you p
spaghetti softer.

5. Drain, reserving a lit
water to add to the sat
the pasta to the sauce
away so it doesn't stick
as it cools.

JAZZ

ADD
CURRY!

ADD PESTO! 500G

ADD PECORINO

FETTUCCINI
cook 8 min

PASTA

O! 500G

JAZZ PASTA

SPAGHETTI
cook 8 min

ADD CURRY! 500G

JAZZ

PASTA

ADD SALSA!

SPAGHETTI
cook 8 min

PASTA

JAZZ PASTA

MAFALDINE
cook 9 min

JAZZ

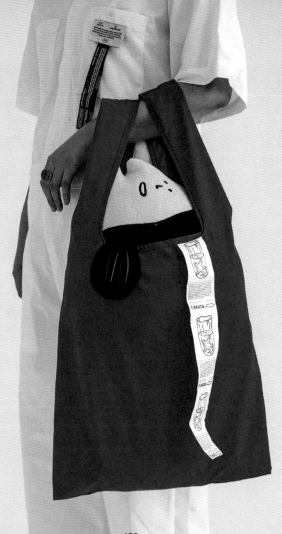

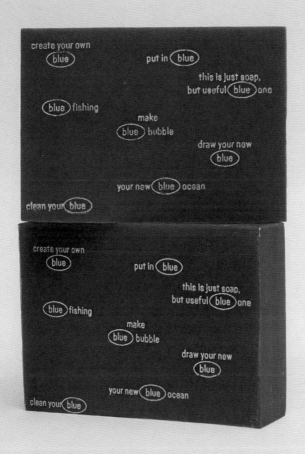

Sundays at

Crown Royal STEPT.

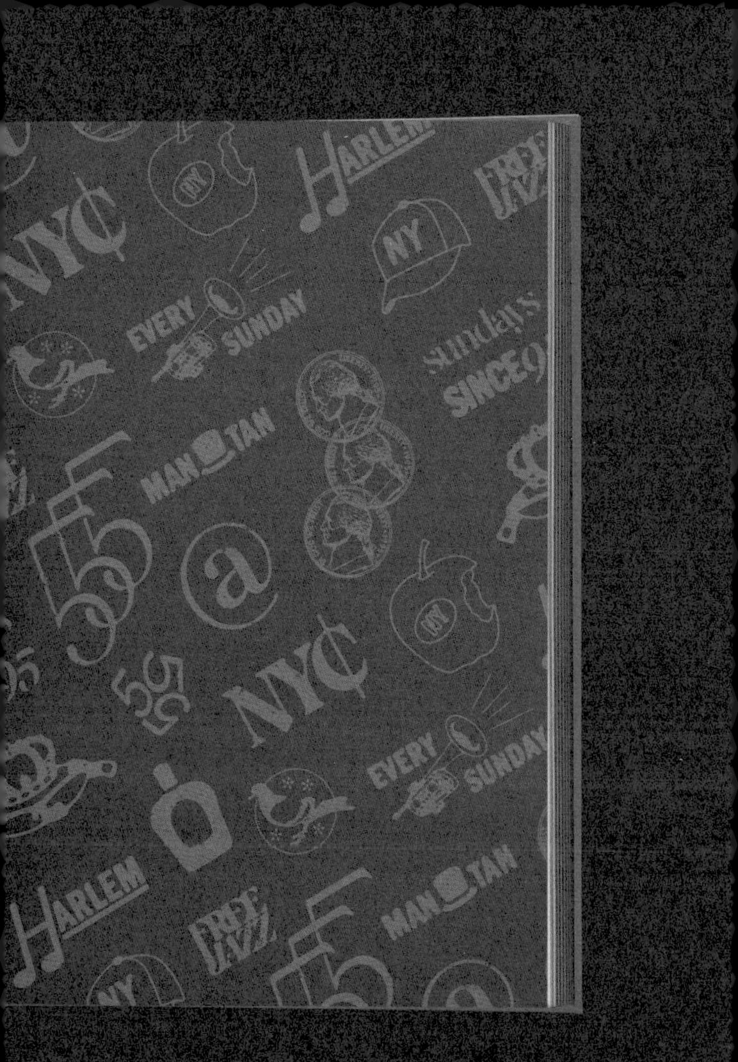
HARLEM
NY
EVERY
SUNDAY
sundays
NYC

Sundays at
THE TRIPLE NICKEL

Crown Royal *presents a* Stept Studios Production
Starring Marjorie Eliot *and* Rudel Drears
Director of Photography Zak Mulligan *Editor* Mattias Evangelista
Executive Producers Nick Martini, Randall Bourquin, JJ Rubin
Creative Director Adam Rachlitz *Design* Lindsay Wallner
Producer Cordielle Street *Score & Soundscape* James William Blades
Written and Directed by Jess Colquhoun

WITH ALL
OUR LOVE

TO BE WED 19 OCT

ROM

AUCKLAND. INVITATION TO

ROMAN JURIS

LYN

N

SAVE THE DATE FOR LOVE

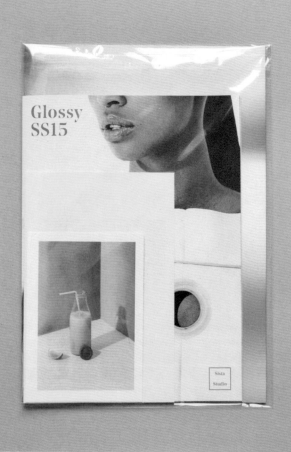

the

WALL
STITCH
PROJE...

— by —

YOY + KS...

wallstitch.com...

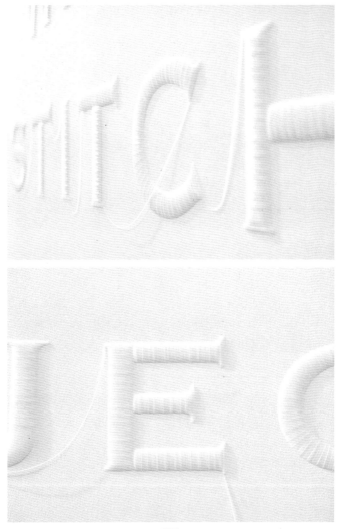

the

WALL STITCH PROJECT

by

" A monotone palette speaks sophistication in a clean and minimal way."

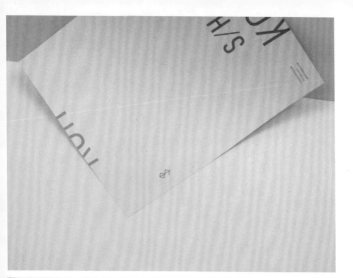

540

541

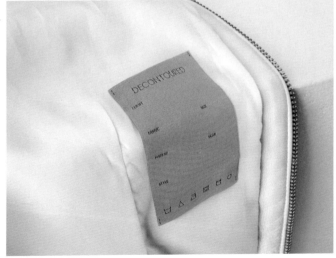

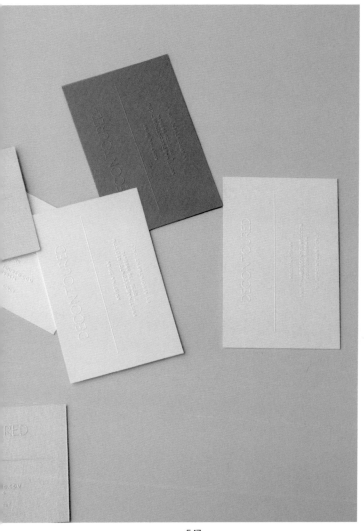

すわさらら
SUWASALALA
ILLUSTRATIONS BY JUNYA MAEJIMA
WORDS BY MACHIKO IWAMAS

はらりるち
HALALILULA
ILLUSTRATIONS BY JUNYA MAEJIMA
WORDS BY MACHIKO IWAMAS

ぽぽぽぱんぽぽ
POPOPAPONPOPO
ILLUSTRATIONS BY JUNYA MAEJIMA
WORDS BY MACHIKO IWAMAS

しゃわしゃわわ
SHAWASHAWAWA
ILLUSTRATIONS BY JUNYA MAEJIMA
WORDS BY MACHIKO IWAMAS

どっががっか
DOGGAGAKKA
ILLUSTRATIONS BY JUNYA MAEJIMA
WORDS BY MACHIKO IWAMAS

じりじじじ
JILIJIJIJI
ILLUSTRATIONS BY JUNYA MAEJIMA
WORDS BY MACHIKO IWAMAS

しゃらしゃら
SHALASHALA
ILLUSTRATIONS BY JUNYA MACHIDA
WORDS BY MACHIKO IWASE

ひららひら
HILALAHILA
ILLUSTRATIONS BY JUNYA MACHIDA
WORDS BY MACHIKO IWASE

550

humancloning.1@gmail.com
www.valchen.com

humancloning.1@gmail.com
www.valchen.com

Blow up

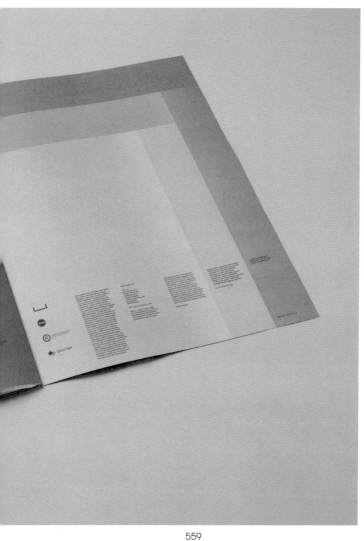

静かなのは、
名前だけにしておけ。

静岡新聞

静岡新聞

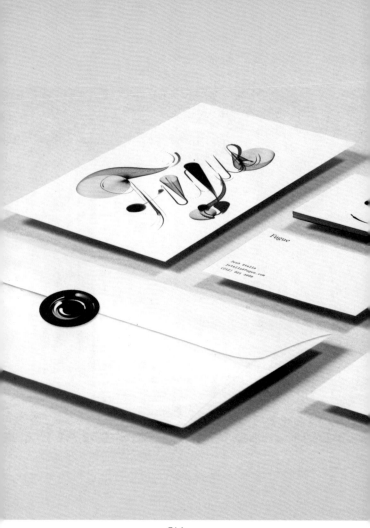

565

Fugue

Josh Stella
jstella@fugue.com
(212) 821 9969

"Monotone graphics are always about doing more with less."

575

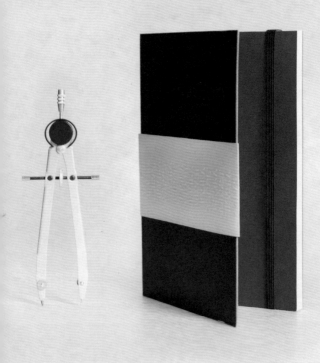

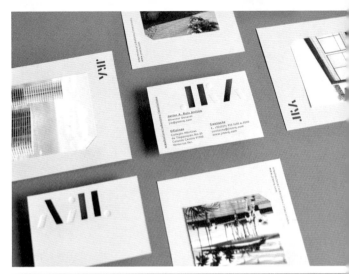

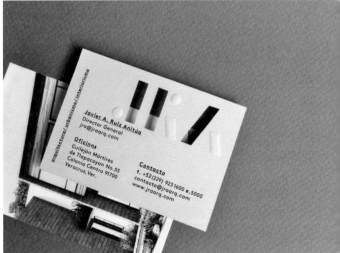

585

제5회 서울레코드페어
5TH RECORD & CD FAIR IN SEOUL
2015. 6. 27. SAT – 28. SUN 11AM – 8PM
한일물류창고 HANIL WAREHOUSE
서울시 강서구 양천로 537
무료입장 FREE ENTRANCE

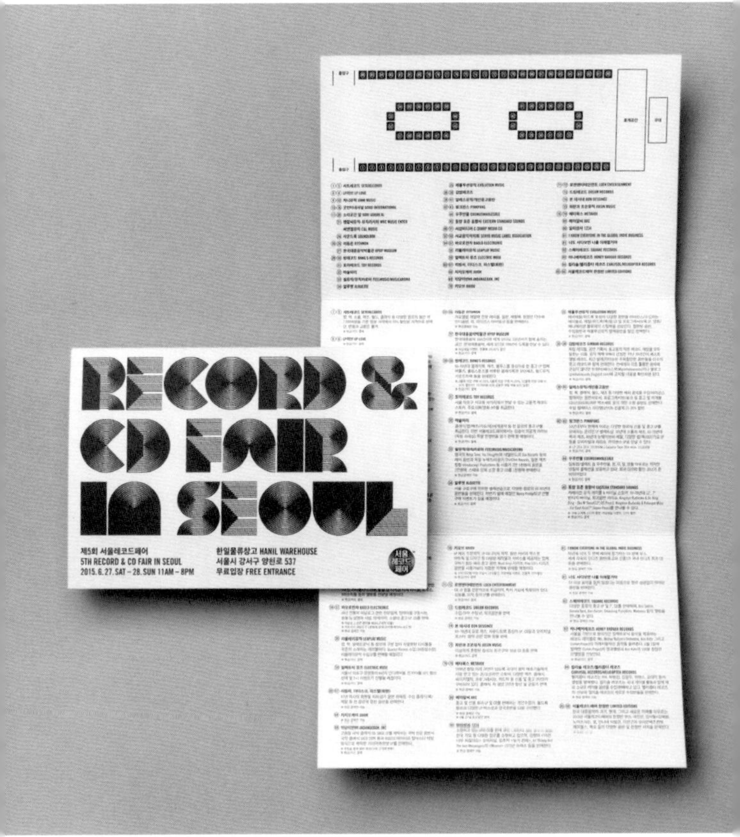
RECORD & CD FAIR IN SEOUL
제5회 서울레코드페어
5TH RECORD & CD FAIR IN SEOUL
2015. 6. 27. SAT – 28. SUN 11AM – 8PM
한일물류창고 HANIL WAREHOUSE
서울시 강서구 양천로 537
무료입장 FREE ENTRANCE
서울 레코드 페어

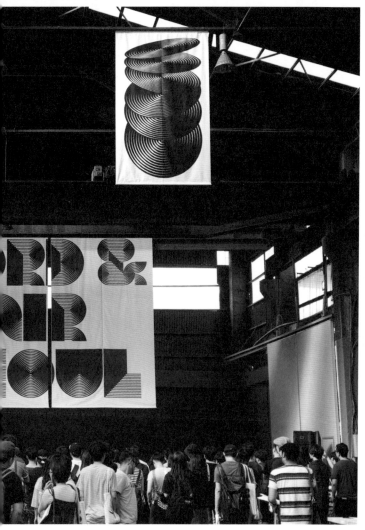

INTERAKCJE

MIEDZYNARODOWY FESTIWAL SZTUKI

MIĘDZYNARODOWY FESTIWAL SZTUKI

GALERIA ODA PIOTRKÓW TRYBUNALSKI

INTER AKCJE
MIĘDZYNARODOWY
FESTIWAL SZTUKI

INTERNATIONAL ART FESTIVAL
ODA GALLERY
PIOTRKÓW TRYBUNALSKI

05-12/05

1 7 2 6 1 3

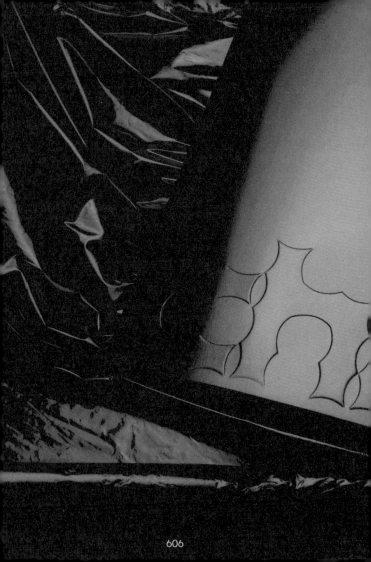

FORTH

GOES OUT IN THE CALM

2019

About

Forth + Back is a mul
Los Angeles CA, found
Together, they view the
problems, both old an
and continually share

Services

Identity Design
Creative Direction
Art Direction
Brand Style Guides
Brand Strategy
Naming

Contact

forthandback.la
hello@forthandback.la
@farmaldbackstudio
+ 1.213.215.1541

Photography
Title Sequences
Campaigns
Signage & Wayfinding
Environmental Design
Illustration

Motion
Print Design
Typography
Web Design
Branding

their curiosities with others.

disciplinary design studio based in East
ed by Nikolos Killian and Tanner Woodbury.
eir studio as a platform to break grounds in
d new. The studio aspires to stay curious

+ BACK

619

+ BACK

Forth + Back is a multidisciplinary design studio based in East Los Angeles CA, founded by Nikolos Killian and Tanner Woodbury. Together, they view their studio as a platform to break grounds in problems, both old and new. The studio aspires to stay curious and continually share their curiosities with others.

Photography
Title Sequences
Campaigns
Editorial Design
Print Design
Packaging

Illustration
Environmental Design
Signage & Wayfinding
Typography
Web Design
Motion

Identity Design
Creative Direction
Art Direction
Brand Style Guides
Naming

+ 1 213 213 1243
@foldmstudio.io
foldmstudio.io

短衣夜行紀

李維怡‧文字耕作

ISBN 978-988-15507-6-7
HK$ 62
PUBLISHED IN HONG KONG

9 789881 550767

《短衣夜行紀》是李維怡繼二〇〇九年《行路難》後於本
地出版的文字耕作結果。集子中,李維怡嘗嘗以文字凝煉
各種社會參與的思考和感受,進一步走向「精詩歌」散
文、紀錄片、小說共融的筆耕方式。集子以真實世界的
現象、蘊藏、紀錄下各種劇場的浸淫,以圖在這急速
消費化、廣告化、偶像化的都市中,持續拷問「人」的
立足點。

雄仔叔叔在序中寫道:
「歷史和瑣事,會被遺忘,甚記不清楚。從一九六六年
的反天星加價事件到二〇〇五年的反韓農收購,途經一
九九七年的金輪大廈天台抗爭再到二〇一〇年的反高
鐵。我們記得什麼呢?除了「歷史的算術」,我們記得
那些人嗎?……在社運抗爭的呼喊、激昂中、理論,
認知只是抗爭堡壘部份的基石,這部份的基石可在權力
運作下不朽壞,只有人與人之間的愛和尊重,才是抗爭的
人間正道……」

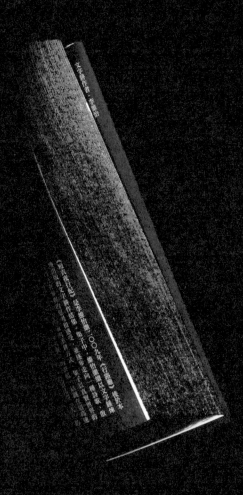

INDEX

BIOGRAPHY

&Larry

andlarry.com

Founded in 2005, &Larry is a design company based in Singapore whose practice is deeply rooted in creating empathic connections between people. It believes that design innovation should always serve human interest – holding a high regard for the intuitive use of data, research, and technology in support of creativity instead of being limited by it.

PP. 046–049, 266–275

7654321STUDIO

7654321studio.com

7654321STUDIO is a design studio that integrates innovation and execution. It provides design and consulting services for clients in the commercial and cultural sectors by understanding contexts, defining concepts, striving for accuracy and clarity, as well as building relationships and experiences.

PP. 136-147

A Work of Substance

aworkofsubstance.com

A Work of Substance uses design as a tool to rejuvenate and create inspiring works of substance in local neighbourhoods. Ever-daring and ever-curious, they constantly venture into new projects and industries through commissions that span the globe.

PP. 460–467

Acmé Paris

acme-paris.com

Founded by Elodie Mandray and Caroline Aufort, Acmé is a Paris-based graphic design studio with a 'will do anything' spirit. Experts in art direction, print, visual identities, and typography, it works closely with clients to add a hand-crafted dimension to brands, combining the infinite possibilities of combinations with the inherent restraint of each project.

PP. 434–439

Akatre

akatre.com

Akatre is a creative studio in Paris that was founded by Valentin Abad, Julien Dhivert, and Sébastien Riveron in 2007. The trio specialises in graphic design, photography, typography, video, artistic installation, and musical creation for institutions in the art, culture, fashion, media, and luxury industries.

PP. 418–419

Anagrama

anagrama.com

Anagrama is an international branding firm specialising in the design of brands, objects, spaces, software and multimedia. It thrives on breaking the traditional creative agency scheme, integrating multidisciplinary teams of creative and business experts.

PP. 010–015, 114–123, 162–165

Apartment One, Inc.

An award-winning strategic and creative agency with years of collective experience working with leading companies and organisations, Apartment One's diverse and time-tested expertise enables it to deliver solutions that reflect a rare synthesis of strategic, creative, and operational thinking, resulting in higher engagement, faster growth, and proven success.

PP. 240–247

Ara Estudio
araestudio.es

Ara Estudio is run by Leticia, Barcelona-based graphic designer and art director who focuses on identity, editorial and exhibition design. Through the lens of fine art and design, she looks out for alternative beauty, character and personality. Her work lies in the cultural sphere, where there is more freedom to create bolder graphics and experiment bigger.

PP. 248–253

Arata Kubota
aratakubota.net

Born in Yamanashi in 1981. Arata Kubota's work has been recognised internationally through awards such as the NY ADC Gold, Cannes Lions Gold, the One Show Bronze, and D&AD Wood.

PP. 166–169, 408–413, 560–563

Atto

Atto is a a design consultancy in Milan led by Sara Bianchi and Andrea Zambardi. It works on a variety of projects spanning brand identities, editorials, illustration, motion graphics and web design. Atto also teaches at schools and workshops.

PP. 390–393

Aya Yagi
ayayagi.com

Born in 1985, Musashino Art University graduate Aya Yagi is a graphic designer and art director specialising in advertising, graphic design, packaging design, and logo design.

PP. 016–021

Baillat Studio
baillat.ca

Baillat is a multiplatform production and design studio based in Montreal that distinguishes itself with an audacious and refined multidisciplinary approach. Closely aligned with the cultural milieus of music and digital art, the studio excels within experimental and conventional paradigms.

PP. 310–313

Blok Design

blokdesign.com

Blok Design collaborates with thinkers and creators from all over the world on projects that blend cultural awareness, a love of art, and a belief in humanity to advance society and business alike. It works across media and a variety of disciplines with a ferocious passion.

PP. 082-087

BLOW

blow.hk

BLOW is a design studio founded by Ken Lo in 2010. It delivers simple and bold ideas with thoughtful details that help brands stand out in the crowd through identities, packaging, environmental graphics, print, publications, and website design.

PP. 096–101

BOB Design Ltd

bobdesign.co.uk

Founded in 2002, BOB Design is a branding and graphic design studio with work spanning across identity, print, digital, environmental, and packaging mediums. Based in London and Zürich, it values research, dialogue, insight, and inspiring ideas.

PP. 060-065

BUCK.STUDIO
buck.pl

BUCK.STUDIO is a Wroclaw-based, multidisciplinary design and consultancy office specialising in the F&B, hospitality, and retail sectors. With international recognition and design awards under their belt, they believe that the best ideas always come from teamwork, where creativity, and consistency are just as important as an open mind, observation, and humour.

PP. 108–113

Bunch
bunchdesign.com

Bunch was a leading creative studio offering a diverse range of work spanning branding, literature, digital- and motion design. Established in 2002 with an international reach from London to Zagreb, it delivered intelligent and innovative cross-platform solutions in communication design.

PP. 544-547

BVD
bvd.se

BVD is the 'world's first simplifying agency'. It believes that everyone needs clarity to stay relevant in a sustainable world. Although it strives to 'Simplify to Clarify', it does not mean that it fears complexity – it embraces it to maximise impact through design.

PP. 198–201

Collins

wearecollins.com

COLLINS is a strategy and brand experience design company with offices in New York and San Francisco. It creates products, environments, and communications that transform brands, drive businesses, and improve lives.

COMMUNE

commune-inc.jp

Motivated by the will to make things better, COMMUNE sets out to encourage a change in society. Based in Sapporo, the creative team specialises in graphic design and creates work that can take people by surprise, awaken their emotions, and move them to tears.

Davide D'Elia

Born in Cava de 'Tirreni in 1973, Davide currently lives and works between Rome and London, producing work that often revalues modern aesthetic terminology and examines the concept of time.

De Intuïtiefabriek

deintuitiefabriek.nl

De Intuïtiefabriek was a design studio finding common ground in their intuitive ways of working, as well as their use of materials and techniques. De Intuïtiefabriek worked to create within different fields of design, aiming to take observers into a new world through their perfectly-crafted products with a pure, precise and almost fragile feeling.

PP. 384–389

Duane Dalton

Duane Dalton is an Irish graphic designer who specialises in logo design and brand identity systems. Minimalistic qualities are often employed throughout his work to communicate a clear and precise message. He is a designer at the London-based design studio SOCIO, but is also available for independent projects.

PP. 582–585

Edited

edited.hk

Founded in 2011 by graphic designer Renatus Wu, Edited is a design studio that works across a variety of mediums. It specialises in publication, identity, and print design – showcasing a clean and minimalist approach through its thoughtful creative output.

PP. 622–624

Edith Rose Studio

edithrose.com.au

Edith Rose Studio was born out of the desire to bring a high fashion aesthetics to wedding and event stationery. Their work focuses on the development of distinctive, thoughtful design solutions that capture each client's personality. Skilfully handcrafted, all pieces are created using traditional letterpress and hot foil printing techniques.

PP. 512–515

Emily Rand

emilyrand.bigcartel.com

Emily Rand is a children's book illustrator based in London. Her first book 'A Dog Day' was published by Tate after being selected for the 2012 Bologna Book Fair exhibition in 2012. She has since written and illustrated picture books with Tate, Thames and Hudson and Hato Press.

PP. 294–297

emuni Inc.

emuni.co.jp

Founded in 2012 by Takashi Murakami and Masashi Murakami, emuni is an art direction and design practice based in Tokyo. The studio is currently in charge of the art direction and graphic design.

PP. 362–367

Eunjeong Kim

eunjeongkim.kr

Eunjeong Kim is a designer in Seoul who specialises in graphic design, branding, and visual identity. She has worked on the Super Matcha branding project and K-pop album packaging designs, and hopes to do something bold and new in the near future.

Fabrica Spa

Established in 1994 by Luciano Benetton and Oliviero Toscani, Fabrica Spa is based in Treviso within a space of magical architecture restored and augmented by Tadao Ando. Under its learning-by-doing approach, creative talents from all over the world experiment with contemporary communication by merging different disciplines.

faraway design

faraway.hu

faraway design is a group of graphic, product and motion designers with copywriters who believe that design is not just about nice typefaces and graphics, but the harmony of words and shapes: the connection of meaning and function.

Firmalt

firmalt.com

Founded in 2012, Firmalt was a multidisciplinary design agency providing creative solutions to position brands. The team's methodology of co-creation with clients results in strong visual concepts that communicate clear ideas, add value, and stand out from the competition.

PP. 160–161, 576–581

Forth + Back

forthandback.la

Forth + Back is a multidisciplinary design studio in Los Angeles, founded by Nikolos Killian and Tanner Woodbury. Together, they view their studio as a platform to break ground by aspiring to stay curious while sharing their curiosities with others.

PP. 506–511, 616–621

Futura

byfutura.com

Since 2008, Futura has become an internationally renowned creative studio characterised by its disruptive approach to design, pushing boundaries and taking risks every step of the way. Specialising in branding, art direction, and photography, the studio's vision consistently blurs the lines between different disciplines, paving the way to new forms of creativity.

PP. 128-135

Gerard Marin

behance.net/gerardmarin

A graphic designer based in Vilanova i la Geltrú, Gerard Marin focuses on visual identities and design solutions that solve communication problems with an element of surprise.

PP. 404–407

Glasfurd & Walker

glasfurdandwalker.com

Glasfurd & Walker provide strategic design services that focus on brand creation, development, and management. The studio creates strong brand stories, narratives, and creative work that are thoughtful, strategic, and genuine yet surprising, engaging, beautiful, and memorable.

PP. 174–175

Grosz Co.Lab

groszcolab.com.au

Founded in 2008, Grosz Co Lab is an interdisciplinary design consultancy with a diverse creative skillset tempered with strategic insight. The award-winning studio excels in achieving a balance between analytical and inspiration-led design. Its refreshing combination of fact and feeling, as well as empathy and commerce, leaves positive cultural impact that transforms organisations from the inside out.

PP. 088–091

Here Design
heredesign.co.uk

Founded by Kate Marlow, Caz Hildebrand, and Mark Paton in 2005, Here Design is a multidisciplinary design collective in London that specialises in design and strategic thinking for branding, packaging, print, publishing, point-of-sale, products, and websites. The studio has won multiple awards locally and internationally.

PP. 400–403

Heydays
heydays.no

Heydays is an Oslo-based design studio that creates strong visual concepts to trigger curiosity, create excitement and show ambition. They listen, research, and challenge – removing noise to add value.

PP. 182–185, 376–379

Homework / Jack Dahl
homework.dk

A creative agency and design consultancy founded by Jack Dahl, Copenhagen-based Homework specialises in brand expressions, visual identities, and packaging within the luxury and lifestyle industries. Once an art director for international men's fashion magazines, Dahl has also worked with the world's most prestigious style, beauty, and luxury brands.

PP. 212-215

Hye-min Jung

Hye-min is a Hongik University graduate designing from Seoul.

PP. 474–477

---

id inc.
id-inc.jp

id is a Japanese design office that was founded in 2013 by Seiji Oguri and Yohei Oki. It deploys design in a wide variety of fields, including graphics, products, interiors and architecture.

PP. 342–351

Inhouse
inhousedesign.co.nz

Founded in 1995, Inhouse is an Auckland-based consultancy that creates appropriate and effective solutions through simple, clear, and well-crafted graphic design. The studio often collaborates with other creative specialists such as artists, architects, product designers, and digital experts to enhance its clients' businesses through design.

PP. 420–423

Julia Kostreva Studio

juliakostreva.com

California-based graphic designer and art director Julia Kostreva studied at the Maryland Institute College of Arts before founding her own creative studio. She works closely with brands to create limited-edition home goods and accessories.

PP. 186–193

Junya Maejima

junyamaejima.com

Born in the Ibaraki prefecture in 1986, Junya Maejima joined Nippon Design Center Inc. after graduating from the Department of Science of Design at Musashino Art University in 2009.

PP. 548–551

Juri Okita

juriokita.com

Juri Okita is a Japanese graphic designer who focuses on creating brand identities. Currently working independently with start-ups to help them craft the visual language that will define their core messaging, she has previously worked with teams in NY and Tokyo on a variety of projects.

PP. 330–337

Kevin Lucbert

kevinlucbert.com

Born in 1985 in Paris, Kevin Lucbert is a French artist and illustrator who received his diploma in 2008 from the National School of Decorative Arts of Paris. Today, he lives and works between Berlin and Paris. A member of the artist collective The Ensaders, he also conducts drawing workshops and participates frequently in various exhibitions.

PP. 468–473

Kokoro & Moi

kokoromoi.com

Kokoro & Moi, established in 2001, is a full-service creative agency transforming brands with bold and progressive ideas. They focus on strategy, identity, and design by being inquisitive and challenging norms, seeing each project as a unique collaboration to craft authentic, imaginative solutions that make an impact on products and environments.

PP. 276–281

Kuhnrae Wu

Born in 1992 in Guangzhou, Kuhnrae graduated from the Guangdong Industry Technical College after a year of studying in Taiwan KSU. He is currently working as a designer.

PP. 176–181

Luca Ricci

behance.net/lucaaricci

Luca Ricci was destined to become a surgeon, but was convinced by a family friend to switch paths before starting his medical studies – and also his future. He subsequently attended the European Institute of Design in Milan to let his creativity flow.

M35

m35.com.au

M35 is an international design consultancy based in Sydney. It partners with ambitious clients to launch and reimagine brands on a global scale. Using a research-driven, human-centric, and holistic appoach, M35 accelerates growth through origination, identities, products, packaging, publishing, physical environments, and beyond.

Marcel Häusler Grafik

marcelhaeusler.de

Marcel Häusler designs visual identities, publications, and posters with a focus on typography. He currently works as design director for Karl Anders based in Hamburg and Paris.

Matilda Saxow

matildasaxow.com

Matilda Saxow is a Swedish graphic designer and art director predominantly engaged with editorial design and branding projects for the cultural and commercial industries.

PP. 234–239

MAUD

maud.com.au

A D&AD-winning design studio based in Sydney, MAUD is as passionate about the core idea as the images they create. The studio continually strives for creative excellence through consultation, collaboration, and detailed execution.

PP. 022–025, 556–559

Michael Boswell, Elle Kim

Michael and Elle are two part-time collaborators living and working in New York City.

PP. 538–543

Michelle Tiquet

behance.net/mtiquet

Michelle is a freelance graphic designer in Mexico City who specialises in set design, branding, and editorial design. She believes in creating images that communicate things in a straightforward way without the unnecessary paraphernalia, but are still fun, dynamic, and captivating.

PP. 032–035

Misawa Design Institute

misawa.ndc.co.jp

Born in Gunma in 1982, Musashino Art University graduate Misawa worked for nendo and Hara Design Institute at Nippon Design Center in 2009, before founding the Misawa Design Institute in 2014. His work encompasses many fields including graphics, products, and space planning.

PP. 532–537

Mubien Brands

mubien.com

Mubien is a full-service branding studio focused on helping companies become fully themselves. It blends simplicity with sophistication to create elegant, powerful and timeless identities.

PP. 036–045

Murmure

murmure.me

Based in Caen and Paris, Murmure is a creative communications agency specialising in strong visual identities. Led by art directors Julien Alirol and Paul Ressencourt, it produces singular and original creative projects, with aesthetics adapted to its customers' problems.

PP. 502-505, 612-615

NOSIGNER Inc.

nosigner.com

NOSIGNER is a social design company actively driving social changes toward a more hopeful future. The term NOSIGNER translates as professionals recognizing the "unseen" behind the "form" (NO-SIGN). We see design as a tool that enables us to form the best relationships.

PP. 148-153

Office of Demande Spéciale

demandespeciale.ca

Demande Spéciale is a Montréal-based graphic design studio whose speciality lies in building brand identities. Based on exchange and collaboration, it offers contemporary solutions focused on arts, culture, and experimentation.

PP. 424-427

Paul Marcinkowski

behance.net/kaplon

Founder of Unifikat Design Studio, which focuses on details, visual cleanliness, and cohesion leading to elegance, Paul Marcinkowski is an art director and designer with a passion for graphic design, editorial design, and photography.

PP. 594–601

Pin-Kai Chuang

behance.net/bindesignmfba7

Graphic designer Pin-Kai Chuang was born in 1998 and majored in commercial design at the National Taiwan University of Science and Technology. His work has been recognised and awarded internationally.

PP. 222–227

PlusX

plus-ex.com

Plus X is a brand experience marketing and design partner that provides consumers with value through consolidated online and offline designs based on a consistent brand strategy. The team believes that key messages and service functions can be effectively delivered when media channels meet strategic marketing.

PP. 154–159

ReflexDesign

reflexdesign.cn

ReflexDesign believes that the nature of a brand is a conditioned reflection established from its consumers' specific demands. Using innovative ideas, it focuses on creating integrated experiences through visuals, the environment, behaviour and tone.

SAFARI inc.

safari-design.com

Tomoki Furukawa and Jun Ogita founded SAFARI inc. in 2003 to explore the meaning of 'safari', or 'adventure' in Arabic through creative design. Undertaking projects in corporate or product branding, editorial, web and space design, the company produces visuals that exemplify adventurousness with their collective desire of 'cherishing curiosity forever'.

Sagmeister & Walsh

sagmeisterwalsh.com

Sagmeister & Walsh was the design partnership of Stefan Sagmeister and Jessica Walsh in New York City. Currently, Jessica Walsh is the founder and award-winning creative director of her own design firm, &Walsh, while Stefan continues to be a graphic designer, storyteller, and typographer who has designed album covers for renowned musicians.

SDCO Partners

sdcopartners.com

SDCO Partners is a multidisciplinary studio of designers, developers and thinkers. The team comprises listeners and storytellers who combine imaginative ideas with thoughtful design solutions to craft and cultivate brands.

PP. 368–375

Seachange

seachange.studio

Seachange is a full-service creative agency based in Auckland. The team strives to transcend categories, challenge perceptions and endure, combining multiple disciplines like branding, packaging, digital, art direction, and book design for a diverse range of clients.

PP. 072-075

Sista Studio

sistastudio.com

Sista Studio is an experimental creative workshop curated by two French sisters, Amandine Armand and Lisa Armand. While both are art directors, Amandine is fashion-based and Lisa is graphic-based.

PP. 520–523

Studio AH—HA

instagram.com/studioahha

Founded by Carolina Cantante and Catarina Carreiras in 2011, Studio AH—HA is a graphic design and communication studio that focuses on brand strategy, visual identities, advertising, new media, photography, product design, and illustration. With different collaborators, they turn their clients' ideas into fresh and engaging messages

PP. 076-081, 170–173, 568–575

Studio Brave

studiobrave.com.au

Studio Brave is a branding and design studio based in Melbourne that helps businesses transform and grow. Underlined by a determination to differentiate, it combines passion with purpose to 'work for organisations, but design for people'. Its portfolio spans a diverse range of sectors.

PP. 066–071

studio fnt

studiofnt.com

Studio fnt is a Seoul-based graphic design studio that was founded in 2006. The team collects fragmented and straying thoughts to organise and transform into relevant forms. Partners Heesun Kim, Jaemin Lee, and Woogyung Geel enjoy collaborating with other creatives to bring various projects to life across different mediums and platforms.

PP. 092–095, 586–593

Studio Makgill

studiomakgill.com

Founded in 2007 by Hamish Makgill, the independent Brighton-based design studio works with businesses and cultural organisations large and small. Focusing on the creation of brand identities and visual communication, StudioMakgill provides succinct, innovative, beautiful solutions that last, inspire and enable clients to realise their ambitions.

STUDIO NEWWORK

studionewwork.com

A branding and creative studio based in New York, STUDIO NEWWORK assembles passionate type designers with a commitment to excellence in design. Besides working across a range of media spanning print, screen graphics, products, and environmental design, it has also published NEWWORK MAGAZINE, a large-format arts publication.

Studio Ongarato

studioongarato.com.au

Studio Ongarato is a multidisciplinary design studio with a portfolio of award-winning work, built on creative collaboration, strategic thinking and a holistic approach to design. Awarded Studio of the Year in 2017 by AGDA Design Awards, the studio is committed to innovation and bold thinking.

Studio Sly

studiosly.com.au

Studio Sly is a boutique design studio in Melbourne with a focus on branding. Led by independent designer Lauren Finks, it explores brand and bespoke design, as well as the use of unusual materials and experiences.

PP. 054–059

Studio Wedesignstuff

wds.si

Wedesignstuff is a design studio specialising in brand development. It creates design solutions that are instantly recognisable, empowering brands to communicate with their audiences in a more meaningful way. The team loves clear, clever, and highly functional visuals, but do not shy away from playfulness and bursts of colour.

PP. 318–323

Studio Woork

studiowoork.com

Studiowoork is a Jakarta-based design studio that constantly explores the boundaries of creativity through work underlined by great value and strong concepts. It believes that design can be turned into something fresh, contemporary, and bold.

PP. 446–453

Studio8585

studio8585.com

Studio8585 is a creative practice dedicated to producing elegant and impactful solutions by utilising graphic design, art direction, and creative consulting. Its process combines extensive industry knowledge, thoughtfulness, and intuition in creating ideas that endure and make a difference.

PP. 254–259

Thobias Studio

The studio of ESAG Penninghen graduates Thibault Priou and Jonas Obadia, the two art director-graphic designers and photographers are especially passionate about typography and editorial design.

PP. 298–299

TINGANHO.INFO

tinganho.info

Ting-An Ho is an award-winning graphic designer and art director. Besides being one of the most influential designers in Asia, he has also received international recognition and awards. He spends most of his time dealing with cats.

PP. 552–555

Tsto

tsto.org/

Tsto is a graphic design agency based in Helsinki and New York that focuses on visual concepts and art direction. It tackles assignments by disassembling to the essentials, and building them back in a new way that best serves the purpose. It brings ideas to life with the team's varied skillset and the best-suited tools.

PP. 124–127, 282–287

TUKATA

tukata.kr

TUKATA® is a lifestyle brand that looks at common, daily objects via new perspectives that deliver more value to customers through quality handiwork and service. By expanding its collection of novel experiences, TUKATA hopes to create a happier tomorrow.

PP. 490–501

Twice

twice-studio.com

Founded by Fanny Le Bras and Clémentine Berry, Twice is an art direction and graphic design studio based in Paris working mostly in the fields of music, fashion, art, and events.

PP. 428–433

Typical. Organization
typical-organization.com

Founded in 2013 by Kostas Vlachakis and Joshua Olsthoorn, Typical is an Athens-based studio working internationally on typical matters. The team advocates not adding new surfaces to existing ones, but rather aspire to discover the 'typical' structure of a relevant subject.

PP. 194–197

UMA / design farm
umamu.jp

UMA/design farm was founded by art director and designer, Yuma Harada, in 2007. Originally an architecture major, Harada launched the creative unit, called archventer, with Shin-ichiro Masui in 2003. UMA/design farm offers visual solutions from book design and graphic design to exhibition and space design, as well as total art direction.

PP. 050–053

Valeria Obrazkova
behance.net/obrazkova

Valeria is a graphic designer from Moscow whose work ranges from packaging to editorial design.

PP. 484–489

Vrints-Kolsteren

vrints-kolsteren.com

Founded by Fanny Le Bras and Clémentine Berry, Twice is an art direction and graphic design studio based in Paris working mostly in the fields of music, fashion, art, and events.

PP. 602–611

Werklig

werklig.com

Werklig is an independent brand design agency in Helsinki that builds brand strategies and visual identities. Its mission lies in helping clients to conquer the world and designing with purpose, underlined by the belief that brands must be built on truth, not fake stories.

PP. 414–417

Will Kinchin Design

willworks.co.uk

Will Kinchin is an award-winning multidisciplinary designer who has worked for top London design studios, building up a rich body of work along the way. Over the years, he has scribbled, art directed, illustrated, and written for clients of all shapes and sizes.

PP. 102–107

WWAVE DESIGN

wwavedesign.com

WWAVE DESIGN specialises in brand identities, campaigns and product packaging. It provides rigorous, brand-new designs and consultation services for customers in both the commercial and cultural fields, winning over 200 design awards from around the world along the way.

PP. 394–399

YOY

yoy-idea.jp

YOY is a Tokyo-based design studio headed by Naoki Ono, a spatial designer, and Yuki Yamamoto, a product designer. Founded in 2011, it creates new stories between spaces and objects.

PP. 524–531

Acknowledgements

We would like to specially thank all the designers
and studios who are featured in this book for their
significant contribution towards its compilation.
We would also like to express our deepest gratitude
to our producers for their invaluable advice and
assistance throughout this project, as well as the
many professionals in the creative industry who were
generous with their insights, feedback, and time.
To those whose input was not specifically credited or
mentioned here, we truly appreciate your support.

Future Editions

If you wish to participate in viction:ary's future projects
and publications, please send your portfolio to:
we@victionary.com

According to the Cambridge Dictionary, the word 'palette' may refer to the range of colours that an artist usually paints with on a canvas. Today, however, more than just the primary means of creative expression for wielders of the physical brush, its role has expanded to include that of an important digital tool for crafting meaningful solutions in design. On top of manifesting pure works of the imagination as it has always done, the palette has become a purveyor of infinite visual possibilities with the power to bridge art and commerce. Since the release of its first edition in 2012, viction:ary's PALETTE colour-themed series has become one of the most successful and sought-after graphic design reference collections for students and working professionals around the world; showcasing a thoughtful curation of compelling ideas and concepts revolving around the palette featured. In keeping with the needs and wants of the savvy modern reader, the all-new PALETTE mini Series has been reconfigured and rejuvenated with fresh content, for all intents and purposes, to serve as the intriguing, instrumental, and timeless source of inspiration that its predecessor was, in a more convenient size.

INTRO